"Fifteen years of civil war dev
After twenty years of prayer,
training and multiplication of c.. ..ational pastors and churches.
Something is happening here in Liberia that is beyond what we
have could ever have hoped for through our Christian leaders being equipped through GBTF. God has empowered us from within
our own borders!"

—James Togba
Field Coordinator, African Baptist Mission of Liberia

"In the wake of our national genocide in 1994, I personally assisted our churches in replacing slain pastors with faithful yet
untrained men to carry on scores of devastated churches. In 2012,
I was introduced to Dr. Snavely, and the Global Baptist Training
Foundation, who believes in the power of training nationals. The
equipping and empowerment of our indigenous leaders have eter-
nally transformed our movement."

—Denys Rutayigirwa
President and Legal Representative, Baptist Union of Churches in Rwanda

"As a native Christian and minister in Myanmar, I have come to
recognize that our national believers must assume responsibility
for reaching our nation for Christ. We can no longer depend on
or expect Westerners to come and evangelize our culture as effectively as we can ourselves. The time has come for us to reach our
own nation with the gospel. With organizations like Global Baptist
Training Foundation to assist us with preparation, our pastors are
starting new church plants among our people in the north."

—Thang Dong Lian
pastor, Biblical Baptist Church, Yangon, Myanmar

"Paul told Titus to appoint elders in every city on the island of Crete. . . . Two thousand years later, God's plan to reach the nations still hasn't changed! There is still an urgent need to train local, indigenous church-planting pastors who can carry the gospel message most effectively among their own people. This much-needed book sounds a clear call to align our twenty-first-century missionary strategies with the strategy seen in the pages of the New Testament. This is a book every pastor and missions pastor should read!"

—Scott Wilson
Lead Pastor, First Baptist Church, Melbourne, FL

"Every church must be committed to local and global missions, taking the gospel to our neighbor and the nations. Dr. Bruce Snavely knows what it takes to get the gospel to those all over the world. This book is an excellent resource for pastors and those in the pew with a heart for world missions. It clearly shows why and how to equip local leaders to plant and pastor churches. I highly recommend it!"

—Kyle Mercer
Lead Pastor, Two Cities Church, Winston-Salem, NC

# Indigenous

# Indigenous

Missions Aimed at Training
National Pastors Globally

*by* Bruce Snavely

*foreword by* Michael Woodward

WIPF *&* STOCK · Eugene, Oregon

INDIGENOUS
Missions Aimed at Training National Pastors Globally

Wipf & Stock
An Imprint of Wipf and Stock Publishers
199 W. 8th Ave., Suite 3
Eugene, OR 97401

www.wipfandstock.com

PAPERBACK ISBN: 978-1-5326-9910-8
HARDCOVER ISBN: 978-1-5326-9911-5
EBOOK ISBN: 978-1-5326-9912-2

Manufactured in the U.S.A.              NOVEMBER 19, 2019

# Contents

# Foreword

I NEEDED TO READ THIS book. As I took time to reflect on what I read over the weekend, I'm still weighing its message.

As a pastor I have tried to imagine what ministry might look like if I had no pastoral training at all. What if that opportunity was virtually absent?

As a pastor I also tried to imagine someone else from a totally different culture coming in to shepherd the people of our church: learning the language, figuring out the customs, translating the Bible, and leading, all without drawing the suspicion of those around them.

Then I reimagined all of this using the ideas Dr. Snavely reflects on in this book. What if someone offered the practical wisdom and the doctrinal foundations of our faith to someone who actually lived in that very culture in order to reach it with the gospel? What would it look like if we taught and equipped pastors who lived out their faith right in their own neighborhoods?

Now, let's be clear—this is no attempt to supplant the previous pioneer mission philosophy we have historically carried out. Rather, this book offers a refreshed biblical vision that must be pressed for consideration. It is about striking a balance between the pioneering model upon which we have relied and one of reaching existing national believers to exponentially advance the gospel. While reading, I wrote down three towers that challenged me.

The first one is the concern Dr. Snavely demonstrates for Christ's Great Commission churches to extend their greatest reach. The training of indigenous believers is one of the most neglected resources in the twenty-first century. Are we extending our greatest reach as equippers, organizers, teachers, and churches? Is our vision for this reach wide enough, real enough, and really potent enough?

The second tower is the concern Dr. Snavely has for diminished pastors who are on foreign fields serving beyond their educational reach. I am humbled by the turnout of pastors who flock to training opportunities when offered. There is a great thirst among the nationals not merely focused on a desire for learning, but their great desire for leading. They aren't necessarily looking to become scholars but longing to be more effective shepherds.

And lastly, Dr. Snavely directs us to reconsider and reframe our own concern for cultures who are without Christ and are simply beyond our reach. "Here I am, send me, I will go" has been reshaped to "Train me where I live and send me, I can go . . . because I already know the language, the culture, and our people."

Indigenous is indeed a call to rethink global missions.

—Michael Woodward
    Lead Pastor
    Ocean State Baptist Church
    Smithfield, Rhode Island

# Introduction

MY SON-IN-LAW PLAYS HOCKEY on the weekends to unwind from his business demands. On one of those weekends the team goalie suffered a cardiac situation that left him with mere moments to live while on the ice. An ambulance was called, but without immediate intervention the man had no hope of living. Just before he perished in front of his entire squad surrounding the goal crease, a cardiac specialist who was playing on the opposing team stepped forward and began life saving measures. He performed an on-ice procedure sufficient to allow the victim time to get to the local hospital where he had immediate surgery ultimately giving him a second chance at life. However, without that doctor on the ice at just that time, the young man would never have made it to surgery. Thankfully, because God had someone on the scene to minister to this man's urgent need, his life was graciously spared.

What you are about to read about training nationals is predicated upon the same principle. All over the globe are hundreds, if not thousands, of indigenous believers in Jesus Christ who are present and capable of reaching their families and friends with the gospel of Jesus Christ. They already know the language, understand the culture in which they live, and care deeply about the destiny of those around them. With training and minimal support, nationals are positioned to offer immediate and effective ministry.

We are at a crossroads in Christian missions. At this time and place in Christian history, I have come to believe, and I hope you will agree after reading this book, that change is needed to bring balance to our present models. While I am certainly not advocating disposing of traditional mission work, I believe a fresh biblical approach is necessary if the local church is to fulfill the Lord's vision for reaching his world with the gospel.

Everything that Jesus began to do with his earliest followers was rooted in the essential preparation of local leaders to lead churches. Jesus did this with his disciples, and the Apostle Paul did it with his own missionary associates. We would do well to look at and follow this model. This is one story of how this approach is transforming *missions* around the world.

# CHAPTER 1

# Why Our Mission Began

IN THE VAST MAJORITY of evangelical churches today we have become skewed in both our understanding and execution of doing mission work concerning the scriptural mandate of taking the gospel around the world. For over two hundred years in America our concept of doing missionary work consisted primarily of sending trained western personnel to the farthest reaches of the planet to establish a Christian witness among the heathen. There is no doubt that this conceptual model worked and will essentially continue to work among the unreached people groups who remain in need of hearing the gospel for the very first time.

However, after over two centuries of sending missionaries around the world we have reached the place where we now have many indigenous Christians pocketed in many nations who need to be utilized in not only reaching their own populaces, but also challenged and equipped to go beyond their respective boundaries with the gospel of Jesus Christ.

Having been in foreign church planting for over twenty years coupled with teaching in American Bible colleges, my focus kept going back to those who didn't even have access to education, much less, the resources to pay for it. I asked the Lord to direct my steps forward in making this desire missional. Later that year I was unexpectedly invited to train some pastors in the Transylvania region of Romania. The rural areas outside of the larger cities were filled with some of the poorest people in Eastern Europe. Their churches reflected that economic profile but spiritually, they were anything but poor. I was introduced to pastors who had little training to support the demands of their congregations. After returning home to my teaching responsibilities, I became convinced that training these kinds of pastors was going to become my life mission. I resigned my teaching post at the college effective after graduation of that year. I also resigned from the church I was leading in Boston effective at the same time.

In January of 2012, Global Baptist Training Foundation was officially born, and on the weekends, I began to visit area churches and present the vision for training national pastors and church leaders in their native countries. By April, we sold our home and bought a smaller home near my children's families in Florida. In June, we moved and had just enough income to buy food and put gas in the car.

Originally, I believed that in order to get into contact with indigenous pastors I would have to reach out to regional missionaries from the US. You see, all of my training and experience had led me to believe that whatever was done for spreading the gospel in nations around the world was basically being done or initiated by Westerners. I believed that without contacting those in the know, I would not be able to move forward in executing the plan to train nationals. However, to date, I have never picked up a phone to make that first call. I will talk about the significance of that fact a little later.

In April of 2012, a former Congolese student of mine introduced me to a native Christian host in Rwanda, and in July of that year I had the privilege of teaching fifty Rwandan pastors who happened to be the replacement pastors for those who had been massacred in the 1994 genocide. In the post-genocide era, they had been picked purely on the basis of aptitude and leadership ability. They had never been trained for ministry but lead churches anywhere from two hundred to 1500 people. I raised the money for that plane ticket, and well, the rest is history. Since 2012, the non-profit entity called Global Baptist Training Foundation (GBTF) has trained over two thousand pastors and church leaders in nine countries on four continents and we have been contacted by native hosts and leaders in several more countries to train indigenous pastors. Most of this traffic has been created by word of mouth, and social media.

What I didn't know then, but what has been increasingly made apparent over the last seven years, is that there are literally thousands of these kinds of indigenous pastors and church leaders in the developing world who through no fault of their own, have never had access to effective ministry training. Even if it was available in the larger cities or otherwise, their economic conditions preclude them from taking advantage of it.

The vast majority of those who live in developing countries, what we have historically called the Third World, can hardly afford to keep food on their family's tables much less buy education. For the vast majority, life does not consist in many choices or a variety of options. Life is about survival in a hostile environment, plain and simple. Without exception, what God has shown us is that in America, we can scarcely comprehend what life is like for hundreds of millions of people who live in general poverty, filth, disease, and hopelessness toward the future.

In the next few pages I want to relate to you what I have discovered through our own organization about training indigenous leaders, and how this model of doing missions allows for an exponential growth potential in building leaders, evangelism, and new churches. It also forces us as evangelical leaders to recognize the need for a potential paradigm change in how we conduct our mission strategies in areas where indigenous leaders both live and work. I believe it is past time that we consider changing the way we understand what this process of doing missions and adopt a strategic plan for training the indigenous believers on every continent where they presently exist.

# CHAPTER 2

# What is the Mission?

I F YOU COULD WRITE one sentence that sums up missions in the New Testament, what would it look like? Would you go to Matthew 28 and repeat one of those authority-packed statements of Jesus, like *go into all the world and make disciples*? or perhaps, *teach them to observe everything I have commanded you*? If that's your response, you have answered the question with fair accuracy. But what would that mission look like? What would the mission of *moving* and *multiplying* the gospel into the future specifically entail for any local church? What would it demand they actually do? What would it cost not only personally but financially? These are all questions which have to be answered at some point along the way in the process of doing missions.

Some of us, perhaps more Evangelicals than we might imagine, have succumbed to the contemporary practice of making missions all about *short-term* mission trips.

Now don't misunderstand me, this emphasis has had a dramatic effect upon thousands of evangelical Christians in the last twenty years. For many of them, these unique excursions opened up the world of missions in ways most people never thought possible to experience personally. Being taken right into the hot center of the world's spiritually impoverished and underprivileged, many individual believers were able to directly participate in evangelism, outreach, and numerous other beneficial projects which impacted countless lives for the kingdom and for eternity. In many cases, however, not so much. I have personally sat and listened to countless testimonies from men and women returning from overseas trips where witnessing, preaching, and church planting were as far from the agenda as chalk is from cheese. I have talked with mission directors who were disillusioned with their own church's missions philosophy, which appeared to them to have gone far astray from the biblical mandate of preaching the gospel to every creature. It seems the core of the problem was the issue that this new emphasis was a form of *gospel light*, or a form of the gospel simply lacking in a real commitment to move and multiply the gospel forward. This lack of gospel presentation coupled with the short term approach and you have encapsulated much of what became known as short-term mission projects.

In many progressive evangelical churches, "missions" is not necessarily about training indigenous leaders, but rather in doing for the nationals what they must ultimately learn to do for themselves. This short-term fix approach is happening on both secular and spiritual levels. Lumpkin remarked that,

> the overwhelming majority of our mission trips are to places where the needs are for development rather than emergency assistance. And development is about enabling indigenous people to help themselves. This requires a longer-term commitment, not the sort of involvement that lends itself to short-term mission trips.[1]

So whether it is the mission of moving and multiplying the gospel forward or moving a building project forward, the mission cannot be accomplished in mere one-week yearly mission trips. That certainly doesn't nullify the potential effectiveness of short-term mission endeavors. The point that we are making here is simply that our short-term efforts must be aimed at coinciding

---

1. Lupkin, *Toxic Charity*, 720.

with much longer and extended goals which reflect our ultimate goal of fulfilling the Great Commission while enabling nationals to fulfill it in the same way. Consequently, Christ's mission takes not only a *lifetime*, it takes *everything* in between, and we must remember that in using the term *development* Lumpkin's reference can be understood as not just about offering humanitarian needs but in enabling the indigenous to extend their Great Commission commitment within their own *Jerusalem, Judea, Samaria, and uttermost part* (Acts 1:8).

Moreover, what many have discovered about the short-term missions model is that it may actually benefit the short-term missionary more than the intended recipient.[2] No matter if the mission of Matthew 28 is being fulfilled by a Western missionary or a national, *short-term* is an oxymoron to the essential cause. The mission requires of us a continuous, ongoing commitment to faithfully pour out of the physical, spiritual and emotional resources we possess, and even then, that doesn't always spell success. Missionary history is filled with lives spent in service where the dividends just didn't seem to match the investment. In some cases, it appeared that the reaping would never come.

I think of the human cost of someone like Adoniram Judson. Shortly after beginning his ministry in Rangoon, Burma, he was arrested and imprisoned for nineteen months in a Burmese prison where he was hung up by his ankles for hours a day laying in filth and human waste. Not long after his release, his first-born daughter, his beloved Maria, died. Shortly thereafter Anne his wife passed away. So overwhelmed with the burdens of death, heartbreak, and emotional stress, Adoniram dug his own grave and sat in a chair beside it for days afterward. Those who knew him questioned if he would ever recover. He eventually did, and the remainder of his life chronicles the career of one of the greatest pioneer missionaries the world has ever known.

In many churches today the short-term missions trip might be about constructing a building, digging a well, clothing orphans, or a hundred other good things that the poorest among us require

2. Lupkin, *Toxic Charity*, 725.

for life. Our Lord even said that so much as a cup of cold water given in his name would be rewarded one day. But, the question that must be answered is whether this is the essence of what Jesus was commanding in his Great Commission. I ask that question because quite often we can obscure or confuse *good* things with either *better* things or the *best* things. In this case, could we confuse the good thing of providing material needs with the best thing of reaching and training disciples of Christ with the gospel? What is the real difference we are making if we fill the stomach of an impoverished soul and he or she still goes to hell?

It is important that we know how to understand and answer that question! I believe there are at least three critical words we must continuously define and re-define when it comes to the average evangelical church today: *ministry, service,* and *mission.* Ministry is what the church does for its members. We are called to minister to one another, to meet one another's needs by helping our widows, orphans, the impoverished within our churches, etc. Some churches do this better than others, but all churches are called to minister to their own people. The office of the deacon is designed to lead in this ministry and normally they are tasked to meet timely physical, as well as spiritual needs of the congregation as they become necessary.

The second word is *service,* and I think it is here where much of what Evangelicals do in the name of missions are missing the essential mark. Service means acts of service which we do unto others in Jesus' name. Service in Jesus' name can be about anything in an effort to help someone. Let me say unequivocally, that this is a good thing whenever and wherever it is done. The problem comes when acts of service are done in connection with the third word, *mission,* but are not done in connection with the gospel or a clear presentation of the gospel of Christ.

*Service,* when it coincides with *mission* therefore cannot just be doing good in Jesus' name. Mission is gospel-centered and focuses on making disciples, planting churches, and training them to reproduce themselves. Great numbers of missions groups are doing acts of *service* globally in Jesus' name which are not gospel-rooted, and make no attempt to preach the gospel in addition to feeding the poor, digging wells, constructing buildings, or educating children. One of the clearest indicators that the gospel is being preached somewhere is the presence of persecution, but acts of service which are not accompanied by the gospel seldom suffer persecution or real hostility. In more than one of our African classroom locations where demon possession is rampant, preaching the gospel is the most violent act one can perform! Without the accompanying power of God, a normal, spiritually unprepared or unprotected person would not survive!

Most people who return from these kinds of mission trips offer glowing testimonies of how these acts have changed their lives, fulfilled them in ways beyond anything they had ever known, and created a hunger to do more acts of service in the future. Once again, let me reiterate that I support acts of service but they should not be confused with the word *mission* unless they are directly connected to gospel proclamation. Jesus' *mission* of preaching the gospel was always accompanied by some form of persecution, hostility, or ill will on some level, and that has not changed in two millennia. At the same time, few will ever get upset at anyone who is simply providing physical needs. The proverbial writer told us that the one with money has many friends (Prov 19:4)!

Just this past year we encountered one of our classroom sites in Rwanda to have a serious issue with one of the buildings associated with our week-long classes held there twice a year. The rainy season had been especially hard during the late spring rains and many of the mountain side homes near Kigali had simply slid down the mountains in mudslides. Over a hundred lives were lost during this period. On the compound where we stay and teach, one building partially collapsed and needed to be repaired. In our country we likely would have torn it down but here they were simply waiting for the funding to make the needed repairs.

As I finished teaching that week of class I took several pictures and sent them back to our social media volunteers and put them up for all to see. I immediately got calls from interested construction-oriented guys who wanted to fly over, spend a week during our next classroom, and make the needed foundation and building repairs. A great plan was coming together as soon as my feet hit the ground at JFK airport in New York. Since I live in Florida, I knew that this was being seriously considered and was going to require my attention, along with some comprehensive planning. I returned calls from interested men and prayed about putting together a construction team who would ostensibly return with me about three months later to work while I taught pastors in a separate facility. I calculated that for the five to six men to buy tickets, raise the money for building materials, hotel, food costs, van rental, along with rental or purchase of necessary tools needed for the job, we would be spending in excess of twenty-five thousand dollars. Within a few days, on top of all the money I calculated necessary for this project, I began to realize all the other potential issues associated with my well-intentioned plan.

The first thing that came to mind was the language barrier. I need a personal translator for everything I do once I step off the plane in Kigali, so what would be the difference with six or more construction workers? They would have to have personal assistance from at least *some locals* who could direct them. They would need to know local building standards, and where to get the proper building materials. They would need assistance in exchanging money, and then paying the people who assist them. They would need translators for every transaction, every question, every problem, every issue that could possibly arise. They would, by necessity have to have someone with whom they could communicate in order to help them in resolving each issue. That is only the beginning! By the time the workers had dealt with all the essential logistical issues involved, they would not have any time left to actually do the work they had come to do! At that moment I realized that what I was actually attempting to do was opposed to my own philosophy of training nationals. Why did I think me and my "team" could do this job any better than those who actually lived there?

I immediately called every one of the interested parties and shared this information with them. To the person, each of them agreed that the locals had both the right and the responsibility to make the repairs on their own building. We decided as a team we would each try to raise the price of a ticket or make a donation to put toward the cost of repairs only. When the next classroom was scheduled, I had the privilege of donating a significant portion of the funds needed for the repair. The difference was that with the donated funds they simply took charge of making the repairs to their own building themselves. Our Kigali classroom can function more effectively because our hosts now have a key facility repaired and operational. The lesson learned from this experience has continued to shape the way GBTF operates in our own ministry in relation to meeting temporal needs.

The fact remains that we cannot change or alleviate the affects of systemic national poverty by simply throwing money or physical resources at the problem, and unless governmental, political, and social structures are both philosophically changed and ultimately transformed through the gospel of Jesus Christ, national systemic poverty will essentially remain unchanged.[3]

We must carefully discern the biblical motivations for fulfilling Jesus' final words as we spend our missions dollars, because once we have successfully lifted these forgotten poor out of poverty, the question remains: Have we equally equipped them to build their lives on the foundation of Jesus Christ or have we simply spared them the fate of temporal misery?[4]

That last question may be the biggest issue of all because if you are like me, you believe that Jesus' last set of directions to the apostles was directed to them as representatives of the church. In other words, the commission was directed to believers who make up local churches anywhere in the world. The apostles themselves would all be dead by the end of the first century, but the church was

3. Grudem and Asmus, *The Poverty of the Nations*, 28-30.

4. According to Yohannan, Only 1/4 of North American cross-cultural missionaries are involved in evangelism activities (such as preaching, translation, church planting, and teaching), while 3/4 are involved in administration and support work (such as agriculture, aviation, community development, literacy, medicine, and relief efforts). See Yohannan, *Come Let's Reach the World*, 63.

promised a continuous existence throughout the ages. For some, that means a universal body representing all believers everywhere. For others, it means a continuous representation of visible churches throughout all of time. But in either case, one fact remains true. Ultimately, every local body of believers is as universally bound to that particular set of directions as were the apostles who heard Jesus first speak those words.

But what does the Great Commission essentially mean? If we attempted to put this set of directions into one brief, memorable, succinct statement, what would it be? How could we incorporate all of what Jesus said into one demonstrable phrase that sums it all up? Can it be done? If we could, I believe that sentence would simply be three little words; but three very important words. That sentence would be: *Train the nationals.*

It's really one of the simplest propositions we could ever devise. It not only incorporates the command Jesus gave his apostles before departing, it brings together the latter teaching of the NT into one clear, and unforgettable directive. For some of us, this single sentence may not make complete sense, or it may be that you have never focused on that element of missions as the primary objective of what we must do on the mission fields of the world. Most of us, if we have grown up in church or have been to a missions conference or two, can quote or at least remember Matthew 28:18-20, "Go into all the world and make disciples of all nations . . ."

In the early centuries of Christian missions the focus seemed to be more about the simple preaching of the gospel to the unconverted masses. This has been true throughout Christian history. But in any country other than one's own, there are language barriers. So without exception, a major component of any missionary outreach is the mastery of the native tongue. This involves two primary issues: the ability to preach the gospel in the native language, and the translation of the Christian Scriptures into the host language. Without those two things missionary progress would remain at a standstill.

It stands to reason that Western churches spent decades sending missionaries to unreached people groups focusing on these two things alone. In a gospel-starved nation, people would have to be reached and trained to some degree before a new congregation could be started. This is what they would have understood in the "make disciples" part of the Great Commission. Once a new local church was begun the missionary would lead that church for a considerable time before turning the church over to a trained indigenous leader. That leader would have to be trained during the time the church was under development so that in a reasonable amount of time that individual could take over the leadership of the church. Once that happened, a Western missionary could focus on evangelizing in a new location, and thus the process would start all over again.

My description here is a fair generalization of the most common method of reaching unreached people groups for the past two hundred years. It certainly doesn't represent the methods of all missionary efforts, but it does reveal the basic strategy. First, you reach the populace with the gospel and then you begin a church plant. Sometimes this process first requires the translation of the Scriptures into the host language. Early missionary efforts all had to face immense obstacles in reaching vast cultures who had never heard the name of Jesus Christ. This is still true today but certainly not to the same degree. The work of the early missionary efforts produced great numbers of indigenous believers in China, Burma, India, Africa, and South America. Today, there are significant indigenous Christian populations in many of these same countries.

I mention the country of Burma, (Myanmar, as the natives call it) because it has entire ethnic groups who have been successfully evangelized while 89 percent of the population remains Buddhist. In fact, I have had the opportunity of speaking in one of the largest Burmese churches in the world recently and took the opportunity to challenge the church to support training efforts to reach their own country. I'm sure you must be asking yourself right now, "Why aren't they doing this already?" Good question! The answer is simple but it is also somewhat complicated.

First, this church I'm speaking of is quite pleased that they have successfully evangelized and taught the vast majority of their own ethnic clan, and frankly, this is a wonderful accomplishment. But that's the problem. They see themselves as so unique among their own population that they are not focused on reaching the remaining 89 percent of the populace. While challenging them, I asked them to focus on praying for training agencies like ours, and invest in the training of their own countrymen.

Now some might be asking about now why we don't just send more missionaries over there. Well, what would ultimately be more effective: sending English-speaking missionaries or training local Burmese Christians? Obviously, if we could train the natives to reach their own, that would be the optimal solution to every missions challenge like this. The locals are already onsite, and they already speak the language and understand the culture. For example, there are thousands of indigenous missionaries in India at present. These thousands of native missionaries are basically equipped to win their own people, disciple them, and train them for ministry. Many of them require ministry training, but why would it be necessary to spend thousands of mission dollars to send a Western missionary family and sustain them there when we may already have Christians onsite who need to be identified and then properly trained? They already understand the culture, speak the language, and love the people. Even if we deemed a certain geographical area to be without a gospel witness, wouldn't it be better to train a native whom God could burden for that area of his own country?

It would be reasonable to consider that among those native pastors there are those whom your church could support or help train in order to advance the cause of Christ. After all, doesn't this meet the requirement of our Lord's commission to us? We are to disciple or train those we reach for Christ so they will essentially replace our efforts with their own, and if Christian nationals are present and willing to be trained, they are the most effective personnel to do the job.

CHAPTER 3

# Missions: What is Your Perspective?

WHEN TALKING ABOUT CHRISTIANITY and what we do to spread the gospel of Jesus Christ, what in particular comes to your mind? If you are anything like me and my experience in evangelical churches, it probably revolves around the sending out of a missionary family to some far-flung nation in East Asia, Africa, or South America. From the earliest months and years of my Christian experience I remember being introduced, in either church or personally, to missionary families who God had burdened to advance the gospel. In our circles it was usually on a Sunday night or Wednesday night.

The missionary would talk about their field of interest, show slides, and then bring a message on a missions theme. The congregation always had a great sense of excitement on these occasions. Sometimes if the presentation was effective enough the church might vote immediately after the service to support their efforts or at least by the next meeting of the church's missions committee. If not, the family would simply move on to the next church on their schedule and do it all over again, sometimes for up to five full years or in some cases more in order to raise the necessary funding to maintain their family on their prospective field.

One of the mitigating factors in today's church environment is the lack of available church service times for presentation. The Sunday night service has been abandoned by many churches in order to provide greater opportunity for families to spend time together in the increasingly busy schedule of contemporary life. The mid-week service is no longer a single meeting in the auditorium but a multi-age and multi-class engagement aimed at offering as much as possible for the diverse needs among the likewise contemporary congregation. Consequently, a prospective missions family will spend much longer vying for the opportunity not only to impact a church family, but also in raising sufficient support for their mission.

After this herculean effort at raising funds for monthly support, the prospective missionary family will then arrange visas and temporary immigration papers, make multiple phone calls with their respective embassies, and finally if they had moved successfully through this process, raise the necessary funding for the moving of their belongings, arranging housing in their new home country, take one or more trips to their new mission field to make myriad personal arrangements and observations, and then ultimately travel with their family to their permanent but not so permanent new home.

However, this process is by no means monolithic. For those missionary families that are supported through a convention of churches, support may be provided through a central clearing house or office where churches send their funds thereby saving families the rigor of raising their own individual support. Churches really can do much more together than they ever could as individual congregations, and that should always be possible without affecting the autonomy of any participating congregation. This method is far easier on the missionary family because it eliminates the necessity of traveling from church to church. It also allows a missionary to focus on the actual mission strategy in devising a workable plan for accomplishing the ministry into which they sense God is directing them.

Whichever the case, the long-term hope of both the family and their long list of supporting churches, family members, and countless other interested parties would be that they would remain on their mission for an extended period of time—perhaps a generation or a lifetime, start a number of churches, train many nationals, and leave their field at retirement or death with a legacy of Christian influence or achievement. That is the hope.

However, that hope is seldom realized in the way that most believers in Jesus Christ expect. The costs of maintaining missionary families can be staggering. The averages vary from between $4500 to $9500 a month. In some areas of Europe, that number could easily escalate higher in some cases, depending on the demands for children's education costs and general maintenance costs in the particular area a family may live. Couple this with the attrition rate of modern missionary families worldwide who don't make it more than five years, or simply don't make it at all, and we can see that all of the effort, investment, and time has resulted in far less than what the cumulative efforts deserve. Up to half of all new missionaries do not last beyond their first term on the mission field.[1] Add to this the fact that we are sending less permanent families or individuals in 2019 than in any previous generation, and it raises the question not only of our stewardship of mission funds, but also of our strategic methods in spreading the gospel worldwide.

As I sat in my office and thought about this in 2012, I wondered what other kinds of global efforts were being made to both reach and train believers in many of the mission fields of the world that had already been reached with the gospel and might be in the position, with the necessary training, to do a greater work in their own countries among their own people. If so, I thought that it should be that we try to strike a more effective balance between the traditional model of sending missionary families to fields like this with a comparative model of *training nationals already in the*

1. Yohannan, *Come Let's Reach the World*, 45.

*field* both to reach their own people and then train them. After all, they already know the language, understand the culture, and love the people.

I instinctively knew that the typical methodology of sending Western families to the farther extremes of both hemispheres with the gospel has been historically effective. It has resulted in the establishment of hundreds of evangelical churches worldwide, and swept millions, if not tens of millions of Christian believers into the kingdom of Jesus Christ. The question I want to raise is whether that particular method can be effectively improved upon or balanced in today's missions culture. Less than one-tenth of the more than seventy thousand North American missionaries are actually working among unreached people groups.[2]

Unfortunately the evidence shows that despite the fact that the indigenous missionaries do 90 percent of pioneer mission work, they only receive 10 percent of the available mission funding. Meanwhile foreign missionaries who accomplish about 10 percent of the pioneer mission work receive 90 percent of the available mission funding.[3]

Let me give an example of what I am talking about. I point again to the example of Adoniram Judson, who was the first American missionary to leave America's shores in 1812. He spent his lifetime in Burma, and left about seven thousand converts and sixty-three separate congregations of believers. He also left the first Christian Bible in Burmese and a Burmese dictionary, both of which remain staples of the Karen Christians in modern-day Myanmar.

Among one of the mountain dialects, the Hakkha-Chin, nearly this entire ethnic group has been reached with a translation done by J. H. Cope in 1912. This was largely done by the Chin reaching their specific dialect, *one at a time*. Despite the apparent success among both the Karens and the Hakka-Chin dialects, there remain over a hundred different dialects and languages,

2. Yohannon, *Come Let's Reach the World*, 154.
3. Finley, *Reformation in Foreign Missions*, 176, 244.

amounting to about 89 percent in Myanmar that remain to be reached with the gospel.

On a recent trip to Yangon (formerly Rangoon) to teach a classroom of local pastors, I asked my longtime Burmese host Luke why he thought that, despite the presence of missionaries in Burma, such a large percentage of the Burmese population remained Buddhist. His answer was both shocking and illuminating. First, he said very matter of factly, "Westerners cannot reach this country of Myanmar." And then he followed that statement with a second equally stunning statement. He said, "The Burmese Christians have not been sufficiently trained and equipped to evangelize their own people over the long term." Needless to say, I really didn't expect that answer. But then it struck me: imagine just what it would take in both physical and financial resources to reach this unreached segment of the Burmese population with the gospel, if we only relied on Western missionaries or personnel! Fortunately, that is not necessary in this case. There are hundreds of strong Evangelicals among this staggering population that can be trained and modestly funded for church planting in large sections of the country. Gordon-Conwell Theological Seminary's Center for the Study of Global Christianity concluded that 5 percent or less of Asian and African clergy have ever had access to any formal Bible education or training.[4] This demands that we both recognize the presence of this potentially powerful indigenous community and equip them to minister effectively in their own context.

However, this lack of indigenous training is not true everywhere Western missionaries have taken the gospel of Christ. Take South Korea for instance: while just 1 percent of the population claimed to be Christian in 1900, today nearly 30 percent of South Koreans claim to be Christian Evangelicals. This is not because of the presence of Western missionaries who have moved in with the intention of starting churches. Well-trained native Koreans are increasingly carrying out the majority of church planting and evangelism among Evangelicals countrywide. The burden of

4. Johnson, "Christianity in its Global Context."

evangelization and discipleship has increasingly been shouldered by the nationals.

China provides a dynamic example of how indigenous believers can produce optimal results in spreading the gospel. Missionaries from Western nations have not been able to get into China for decades to preach the gospel freely. However, the house-church movement in China has exploded in the last forty years with thousands of small congregations being raised up and shepherded by committed Chinese Christians. This movement in China is presently reaching a harvest of souls through the force of its national pastors and house-church members.

Who has ever heard of missionaries taking the gospel to the former Soviet Union? It simply does not happen with the obvious exception of extreme underground operations. There are, however, present-day efforts to train native church planters in neighboring countries to go in and launch churches, but they are certainly not Westerners. Now, that doesn't necessarily mean that access is completely denied, but it does limit access to only those who come in as teachers or with some other skillset which doesn't openly threaten the culture's status quo.

Africa presents an interesting picture of the growth of Christianity. Only nine million Christians were in Africa in 1900, but by the year 2000, there were an estimated 350 million Christians in a population of about 1.2 billion people. There are approximately 150 million African believers who would claim to be Evangelicals among those who identify as Christians. As a continent whose Christian history goes all the way back to the first century AD, Africa remains one of the prime mission fields of the world. The statistics demonstrate that the growth of evangelical Christians has increased exponentially in the last one hundred years.

One of the problems that comes with that tremendous growth is the proliferation of teaching which both damages orthodox Bible doctrine, or at best dilutes it. Consequently, we have discovered that our training of indigenous pastors demands building critical doctrinal areas which are under attack or have simply failed to impact the unreached millions because of simple neglect.

However, despite the systemic problems within global Christian communities, many of these believers welcome the opportunity to be trained and equipped to reach their nations for Christ if given the opportunity. In the past seven years, the training organization I direct has trained nearly five hundred pastors in both east and west Africa and seen those students start in excess of one hundred viable church-plants.

# CHAPTER 4

# Where is the Biblical Model?

I N 2 TIMOTHY, PAUL was writing Timothy, who was leading the church at Ephesus, while at the same time the apostle
was languishing in the Mamertine prison in the city of Rome.
Concerned with the abdication of responsibility of so many believers in Asia to their Christian calling, Paul was challenging his
Christian protégé to rise up to fulfill his own calling in the training of capable disciples. In this case, Paul took the *Great Commission* of Jesus and laid out the terms for how discipleship was to be
moved forward, not only in the great city of Ephesus, but all over
Asia and the world. Paul identified *four key* leadership abilities in
2 Tim 2:1-7 which were needed for leaders training other leaders
who could in turn train others to move and multiply the gospel
into the future. Based upon his appraisal of the spiritual conditions
he notes in chapter 1, the apostle challenges Timothy to think the
following about his own leadership skills so he in turn could raise
up countless leaders to follow in his wake. Paul's first leadership
ability he raises to Timothy is:

Leaders need to be able to oppose spiritual opposition (v. 1).

In Paul's last days just before Nero likely had him beheaded, the forces against normal Christianity were brutal. The apostle had lamented the fact that nearly all of his supporters had abandoned both him and the gospel. Very few were either willing or able to stand against the hostility aimed at their Christian witness. Consequently, Paul tells the young preacher to "Be strong in the grace" of God. This is an imperative both here in the text and for us today. We have to be constantly living in the strength provided by God's immeasurable grace. No matter how visceral the battle may feel, we don't fight in our strength but God's. Why? Because we are battling spiritual powers which, if left to our own devices, would annihilate us in a micro-second. Depending on God's grace, which by the way, is the same grace that saved us, is the primary means of both our survival and success. This first challenge forces us to recognize that grace does much more than just save us. In fact, grace is the very means God has provided for our spiritual sustenance and strength. Through his grace, he is working his supernatural power and nature into our daily world.

But secondly, the apostle follows this first imperative with yet another command:

Leaders need to hand off the baton of leadership (v. 2).

The hope that the Christian faith continues to extend into the future is rooted in the continuous training of other leaders. It's interesting that Paul's admonition to Timothy is made in the context of leaders who had succumbed to pressures or in some cases even abandoned the faith entirely. Paul then says the only way that the faith can have continuous regeneration is to continuously commit it to others who are capable of reproducing others just like themselves.

This second imperative to Timothy essentially means to entrust, as in entrusting to someone something extremely valuable. It identified the gospel faith as something of incomparable cost, and like a baton in the hand of a relay racer, it must not be carelessly handed off, and it cannot be entrusted to just anyone. So Paul qualifies the prospective Christian leader who is entrusted with the following restriction: Trained leaders must be proven to be faithful.

Paul told the Corinthian church in I Cor. 4:2 that it was *required of stewards that they be found faithful.* The most basic characteristic that can be identified in a Christian leader is *character* itself. Without this Christ-like feature, nothing else really matters. This element is not just a static character trait. It's a way of living life. The world is full of the most useful, talented, and gifted people who cannot be depended on to get out of bed in the morning. Timothy's task was to identify leaders who had *proven* they could be counted upon in the middle of chaos and conflict.

For instance, in China, you can be jailed for the crime of simply identifying as a Christian. If you are a leader, you could find yourself in prison for months, and even years. In the Chinese house-church movement, the pastors who are chosen to lead are not chosen simply for aptitude. In fact, in many cases a Chinese leader will not be chosen to be a pastor unless he has proven faithfulness by having been jailed for his Christian witness. In this way, as mentioned earlier, the house-church movement has multiplied exponentially. Paul stakes his claim for Christian leadership on this quality because he knows this is what God requires and this is what inspires believers to greater commitment to Jesus Christ. But there is a second thing required of those to whom we hand off the baton of leadership: Trained leaders are expected to reproduce the content of their training in others (v. 2).

Here Paul directs Timothy to take "the things which you have heard in the presence of many witnesses" and build those into the lives of other leaders. This refers not just to the simple gospel message but the entire *content* of the Christian faith that Paul had originally taught Timothy. The apostle had earlier reminded the young pastor to "pay attention to yourself and the teaching." At this point in Paul's life and ministry to Timothy he is taking that admonition to his ultimate and concluding intention: the need to reproduce *content-driven* leaders perpetually. In other words, the model of ministry is to end up modeling others with a strong doctrinal mindset.

Without a handing off of what we ourselves have been taught, there is no guarantee that the Christian faith will reach the next generation, at least not in the condition in which it was originally bequeathed to us. That is likely why Paul reminded Timothy to pay attention to the *doctrine* he had received. Unless we are careful to pass on precisely what has been the foundational material upon which Christianity has been built in the present generation, the enemy of our faith has been handed a distinct advantage in the generation that follows. In my own family, I was the first person in three generations to publicly profess and follow Jesus Christ, and by God's grace we have been privileged to hand off the faith to both our children and grandchildren. We are in reality only one short generation from the death of our Christian witness if we fail to successfully hand off the baton.

The first three centuries are epitaphs to every succeeding generation that the content of our faith is vitally important to our faith, in fact critical. For instance, if Jesus is not God the Son, equal, eternal, and co-existent with the Father and Spirit, then we have no Savior, no resurrection, and consequently, no real salvation from sin. As an exemplar, we have Athanasius, among many other faithful theologians to thank for seeing to it that the deity of Christ was preserved intact for the future of our faith. That essentially sums up why what we pass on to future leaders is key to Christianity's perpetuity.

The third of these important leadership qualities is found in the third verse, where Paul pulls Timothy into a critical element of pastoral leadership often forgotten or overlooked today by saying *Suffer hardship with me.* This third leadership quality is:

Leaders must know the value of suffering (v. 3).

In reality he says join me in *obedient suffering.* The reason we may call it *obedient* is because the apostle says further, *as a good soldier of Jesus Christ.* First of all let's be clear. No one becomes a Christian so they can suffer. That is not to say no one would become a Christian if doing so meant they would suffer.

It does mean that part of what it means to obediently and faithfully serve Jesus Christ requires that willingness. Anytime a soldier signs up to serve, he or she does so knowing that paying the ultimate price may be required in their country's service, and so it must be for Christian leaders of every description.

In many countries of the world, just naming the name of Christ can result in persecution, prison, or death. However that doesn't give us the entire picture here because the apostle follows this with a purpose statement in the text. He says that *no soldier gets entangled in civilian pursuits, since his aim is to please the one who enlisted him.* Any soldier serving in a hostile environment will tell you that without strict obedience to the commanding officer, soldiers often die or are placed in perilous positions.

Connected with this thought is the idea of *entanglement.* This is a word describing a person who gets caught up focusing on anything but the military objective. If a soldier, any soldier, begins daydreaming about the house back home, the classic car, or the family, he or she may imperil not only their life but the lives of their compatriots. This is the narrowed focus required of a true leader. No leader can lead without a laser-like commitment to the commander's objective, and that will oftentimes involve suffering on various levels. As Christians, Paul promises us in the very next chapter *that all who desire to live a godly life in Christ Jesus will be persecuted* (3:12). No one understands this better than a Christian leader.

In the last section of this text in verses 4-7, the apostle provides the fourth and final leadership ability. He says in this section that in reaching the ultimate objective of moving the gospel forward,

A leader must must possess a singleness of purpose (vv. 4-7).

Paul provides three clear and concise life illustrations to demonstrate this leadership quality. It is something which every successful leader instinctively knows and must practice if the objective is to be reached. The idea is simple: if you forget about the one, single reason you do what you do, you will likely miss the goal.

Paul begins with the soldier, and as we have already discovered, the soldier has to remain focused on pleasing his commanding officer, That one objective is really all a person needs to know. If a soldier forgot everything else but that one thing, there is still the likelihood of accomplishing the mission.

Secondly, we are given the example of the athlete. The athlete trains and trains to win the ultimate prize! However, Paul reminds us that *the athlete is not crowned unless he competes according to the rules* (2 Tim 2:5). The competitors know that unless the rules of the race are obeyed, winning is not possible, despite the talent and skill level of any athlete. We had a demonstration of this at the 2016 Summer Olympics. The American 4x100 men's relay team was highly skilled and qualified to win the gold medal. But unfortunately none of that mattered. Because on one of the legs they failed to hand off the baton in the proper zone, they were *disqualified* from the race and lost the chance for a medal. Our modern infatuation with winning at any cost must not blind us to our responsibility for Christian virtue. For the spiritual competitor, one's *singleness of purpose* is never only about winning, but *how* one wins!

Thirdly, we have the example of the farmer. What is his mission? Is it to fill his barns so he can build bigger ones? Is it to increase his bank account? Hardly! His primary mission has nothing to do with those ancillary issues. The text says the *hard working farmer ought to have the first share of the crops* (2 Tim 2:6). Why? I thought he was supposed to make a ton of money so he can be successful! Right? Not really. If thats what the farmer's objective is, he's pursuing the wrong thing. The first priority of the farmer is just like that of any bread-winner, which is to put food on his own table. The farmer's first mission is to grow crops so he and his family, through having the first share of the blessings, can meet their own needs!

This is the biblical model of leadership which guarantees a future for the gospel and its being moved forward from one generation to the next. It is the model we must continue to utilize in the equipping of nationals if we want to move and multiply the gospel both intact and with exponential results.

# CHAPTER 5

# What Does Indigenous Missions Look Like?

OVER THE NEXT SEVERAL pages I want to paint the picture for you of how each of the teaching opportunities where GBTF now trains actually began. As I shared earlier, the initial intention when first starting the foundation was to make phone or email contact with American missionaries in the various places where we envisioned a classroom. This would, of course, lead to finding the right hosts, the right facilities, and eventually determining the number of national pastors we could find to train in that particular location. Never have I been so completely off target in terms of taking the right path to anywhere! Since 2012, we have never had to make that first call to a Western missionary or send out that first email in search of a finding a target audience.

Even in January of 2012, when we had barely announced our beginning as a 501(c)(3), I was asked to teach a classroom in Romania for a friend who couldn't keep his obligation to go. When I landed in Oradea, I was picked up at the airport by a national host and several local Romanians. From the time I landed until I left the following week, I spent all of my teaching time with Romanians who identified as either Hungarians or Gypsies. I preached and taught in over six churches and various other locations, and never saw one American or Westerner anywhere. In fact, my host, who was a native Romanian and pastored eleven churches, basically took time only to eat and put gas in his car to go to the next village or town. The churches varied in size from thirty members to three hundred members but the thing which characterized them all was the joyful music and simple passion they had for serving Jesus Christ. It was humbling and inspiring all at the same time. Unfortunately, the Lord did not keep that particular door open for the foundation, but that one teaching experience taught me much about what I would encounter as I set out to train national pastors on a global scale.

## Rwanda

Before leaving the college later that spring of 2012, the Lord would use one of my former students to open a very strategic door for GBTF into Africa. I had this dull ache in my gut about the great continent but I had no idea how we would get introduced to our first missionary and subsequent country. As I pondered this one morning on the way to teaching an early class I ran right into my one and only Congolese senior rushing into class as I made my way in the door. He quickly said hello, took his seat, and as I was taking attendance, he raised his hand and told me he had something to tell me about Rwanda after class. I knew that was where a terrible genocide had taken place sixteen years prior but little else.

When class ended he came right up and began to tell me about the need of training pastors in the Congo where he lived as well as the little country of Rwanda, right on the eastern border. He asked me if I would be interested in teaching a weekly module in his small town in the Congo as well as be introduced to an Evangelical Baptist leader in Rwanda. I told me I was all ears and before that week was over he had made both those arrangements. I didn't realize it at the time but this would be the essential pattern for how we would add new nations all over Africa. The only difference would be that we would go from indirect introductions to word of mouth: one African to another, who in turn would reach out to me either through our website or foundation telephone. If they wanted to make contact with us they usually found a way.

Upon making arrangements I had a conversation, well, maybe we could say a very basic talk with the legal representative of the Baptist Union in Rwanda. For the sake of privacy, I will refer to him as Pastor D. He is well-known and respected throughout Rwanda. Before I tell you more about Pastor D, let me give you a little background first. Pastor D was a Tutsi leader like his father had been for many decades. He had become a Christian in the early 70s and had pastored and assisted in the starting of several churches all over the country.

Long before this period there had been and continued to be a growing animosity against the Tutsis by the Hutu tribe. This had been going on for several years and had been carefully nurtured and fostered both in the political and educational systems. By the time the genocide began around Easter Sunday, 1994, the hatred and disdain by the Hutu clans toward the Tusti people had reached a fever pitch that could no longer be held back. The Hutus had death lists which included the names and locations of key leaders and spokesmen who were marked for death on that fateful day in April.

Just the previous evening many Tutsi and Hutu neighbors had spoken pleasantries to one another before retiring for the night. When morning light appeared, the genocide—and essentially the removal of Tutsis by any means possible—was announced by traveling loud speakers mounted to cars and trucks, as well as over radio. Without warning one of the worst murderous genocidal campaigns in history had begun. Pastor D was on one of those first lists and he was sitting in his house early that morning knowing that his enemies were likely to appear at any time, and he was right.

About eight o'clock that morning three Hutu men armed with machetes threw open his front door and marched in across the threshold just as Pastor D was reading his Bible and praying. He told me that he looked toward heaven and knew that he had just moments to live. His wife and adopted daughter were hiding in the back room in a closet. He prayed that they would just kill him and then leave. Before he could finish his prayer, he said there were gun shots outside in the street and his three executioners thought a militia group had come to kill them so they bolted out the door about as fast as they had arrived. Pastor D knew they would be back; he just didn't know when.

Less than two weeks later the same three men, armed with machetes, appeared at his door again. This time he knew they would not leave until it was finished. He braced himself for what he knew would be a painful and tortuous death. When he looked into the eyes of his attackers he quickly noticed that their intensity to kill had been replaced with what could only be described as bewilderment, a total sense of confusion and mental chaos. Then he said he saw the bewilderment turn to abject fear, in fact it seemed so intense that his executioners seemed to be fearing for their own lives, and then finally out of nowhere, his three would-be assassins turned and fled out the door as if they were the ones that were now under attack. Pastor D told me that he was absolutely alone that morning in his empty house. His only explanation for what happened was that, in answer to prayer, the room had been filled with fierce angelic warriors who were far better armed and capable than his potential killers. Whatever they saw in the room that morning they wanted no part of it, and Pastor D was spared for the second and last time.

Three months later in July, Pastor D began a slow and deliberate travel schedule around the countryside by foot and motor-scooter viewing the carnage and beginning to assess both the physical and spiritual horror the country had endured. He witnessed human atrocities that were beyond human imagination even in a normal war event. In an interview I did with a nephew of his uncle's family I learned something about just how awful and perverse the genocide actually was during that brief three month period. On this occasion the uncle's family of six were attacked in their home a few weeks into the horrors when their Hutu killers demanded their money. The father told them he had more money in the bank and that they could have it but it would take him a few days to get it for them. His murderers told him they would be back in two weeks and if they had the money ready they promised to kill them with guns instead of hacking them to death with dull machetes. The word was sent to other tribal enforcers that this family were to be kept from escaping until the return of their killers.

True to their word the family gathered all of their savings at their home until they were met at the agreed time. Their executioners asked the father how he wished his family to die and he asked them to begin with the youngest to the oldest. Their sixteen-year-old son attempted to flee into a wooded area and was caught and returned to the murder scene and killed. The father received his request of being killed last. The nephew told me this was one of the few acts of mercy anyone knew about from the three-month nightmare in Rwanda.

When Pastor D reached one village or city after another he found decimated churches and multiple slain pastors and their families. Immediately he set out to find one or more faithful men who were willing to lead the churches out of their darkness and death. Over forty congregations needed leadership but Pastor D did something that astounded both the survivors of the congregations as well as the government as it attempted to recover in the ensuing months of re-building.

Instead of choosing the pastors from among the Tutsi victims, for the purpose of advancing the principles of forgiveness and reconciliation, he chose leadership from those among the non-participating Hutu tribe, many of which had been killed alongside their Tutsi rivals for being accused of sympathizing with the enemy. Initially Pastor D took great criticism for making such a decision. Many could not understand his thinking or accept the premise of Hutu leadership, even if they personally hadn't embodied the hate which precipitated the genocide. But, as the closing weeks of the summer of 1994 led to the first few years of the new government of Paul Kagame, the president heard of Pastor D's policy of forgiveness and reconciliation and invited him to his office to discuss this ideology as a country-wide policy.

In those first several years of renewal Pastor D was asked to direct several policy meetings where reconciliation based on forgiveness between the warring tribes was the focus. Today, Rwandan law forbids any Rwandan citizen from publicly declaring tribal identity. However, genocidal tendencies do not die easily. Even today, continuous efforts must be made to ensure that smoldering embers of hate are not allowed to turn into open fires of hostility and violence. Therefore, education from the earliest grades include efforts to make sure children are educated to understand racial and tribal tolerance, but it will take decades of vigilance to make sure that 1994 never happens again.

When I first met Pastor D in 2012, he was present every morning of our first week of class and made sure I didn't make any big mistakes in handling the questions from the nearly forty-five pastors present. As the replacement pastors for those killed in the genocide, there were questions asked of me that I could have never anticipated. On the third day of class I opened up for questions and received one that I will never forget.

A pastor stood, thanked me for coming to train the leaders, and then told me he had a man in his church who had escaped being killed in the genocide but his wife and daughter had not been so fortunate. He had since remarried, had children with his new wife, and had carried on as normally as possible. He then said that during the previous year this man's first wife suddenly walked into the village seeking her former husband. Having been presumed dead for well over five years, the entire village was shocked to actually see her alive. The pastor said that she had suffered for several years after the atrocities were over and was simply unable to return. Upon her return, her husband met her and told her about his new family. Now the pastor posed the question he wanted answered. He said, "What should the man do now that his first wife is actually found to be alive?" As I sat there that morning I instinctively knew that I was not simply answering this one pastor's question but also posturing for street credibility with forty-four other pastors listening in to our conversation.

I cleared my throat and restated what the pastor had already told me. The man had remarried with the clear understanding that his first wife had been killed along with their daughter. In fact, the daughter had been brutally killed, but his wife had served as a sex slave and been beaten for weeks until the genocide was over. Everyone, and not just himself, had concluded that she was dead. The decision to remarry was based on sound reasoning but now the husband was faced with a very difficult situation. I confirmed the difficulty but told him that in light of what was known at the time of his remarriage, the second marriage was not only legitimate but God-honoring. The first marriage had to be considered terminated. It was not easy for anyone, especially for the first wife, but the second marriage had to stand. There was a pause when I said that part, but then I felt that the husband's duty to his first wife was not over simply because of these mired circumstances, so I added that he would have to care for her needs until such a time that she could be properly remarried.

With that said, I stopped and waited for the pastor's response. He nodded, seemed to agree with my assessment, and sat down. I signaled the men to take a fifteen-minute break and I immediately looked over to Pastor D to ask him about how he would have answered that question. He laughed and said that pastor asked him the same question a month earlier and he had answered it in exactly the same way. What I learned about training nationals that day has served me well for the last seven years. That is, even the indigenous know how to ask good questions to make sure you can meet them where they are . . . and train them for ministry in their own culture.

On the weekends over the years I have had the extreme privilege of preaching in some of the great village churches. After five years of teaching in Rwanda we brought one of our former female students with us who had committed herself to teaching English and the Bible in one of the local Baptist high schools. Kelsey had always wanted to be involved in African missions since a young girl and this teaching opportunity had presented itself to her less than a year after her graduation from Bible college. She had raised the funding for travel, one year of living expenses, and taken care of all the details of her year-long tenure in Rwanda. That very last weekend before leaving her in the hands of our African hosts I was invited to speak to a group of churches in southern Rwanda. Very early Sunday morning Pastor D, Fidele, Kelsey, and my wife and I were on our way to a church about three-and-a-half hours from the capital city. Once we arrived we had a breakfast inside the two-room block home of the pastor. We then had prayer for the service. Just before heading over to the worship area, I asked the pastor's wife if I could borrow a wet cloth to wipe the dust and dirt off my shoes before I went over to the service. She asked me for my shoes, and then another woman asked me for my shoes. I was a little confused when all of a sudden the pastor's wife literally snatched the shoes off my feet and disappeared for several minutes. I asked Fidele what was happening and he laughed and told me they each considered it a great act of service to clean my shoes and they were fighting over them for the blessing. The pastor's wife won that battle!

The outside meeting that morning was the gathering of three or four area churches who combined their services for this special occasion. It is always humbling to see how Africans prepare for outside services like this one. People will bring large African rugs from their homes and churches to lay over the ground where all the pastors and leaders will be seated. Then they wrap all the tent poles holding up sun coverings with colorful cloth and ribbon. Then as many chairs and benches that are available are set up in rows. When all the chairs are taken, all other attendees stand for the duration of the three- to four-hour service.

That particular morning we had over seven area choirs sing for the service. It is always a real treat to hear and see the various forms of song and dance the Africans use in worship. By the time I got to the pulpit to preach that morning it was nearly twelve o'clock. I spoke for about thirty-five minutes and I noticed while I was preaching a half dressed woman was walking back and forth in front of the pulpit. About mid-way through the message the deacons came and gently removed her and got her to sit down away from the pulpit area. I could still see her from my vantage point. She was visibly irritated and unsettled but remained there until the service was completed. I found out from our host that she was a demon-possessed woman from a nearby village who would often come to the services to disrupt them.

After the service we ate lunch at the pastors's home, and then got a short tour of the makeshift health clinic for AIDS patients and expectant mothers. Then we headed to the vehicle to get ready for the trip back to Kigali. Standing there beside the car were two or three of the pastors with the host pastor, along with the woman who earlier had been parading in front of the pulpit. I thought it was odd that she would be there but there she was, with her head down and with an angry countenance. I thought little of it at the time. She made no real outbursts but her presence was unnerving to some of those gathering around our car. A few minutes later we were on the road headed back to Kigali.

We were all tired by the time we got back so I had our host drop us off at our rented apartment. We talked with Kelsey about the day, the wonderful worship time we had experienced, and of course that in two short days we would be heading back to the States without her. Kelsey is one of the bravest young ladies I have ever had the privilege of knowing and her response to our departure was just what I expected of her. She was excited about what God had been doing in her life, and especially that she had finally reached one of her great life-dreams of being on mission in the heart of Africa. We talked well into the evening until heading off to bed. Monday morning we were due at the American consulate for some paperwork on Kelsey among other important details before we could leave her on her own.

Grace and I were awakened out of a sound sleep about 2:30 AM by Kelsey knocking on our bedroom door. Before I even invited her into our room, I could tell that there was something visibly wrong with her. Her head was down, she appeared to be in a sense of panic, and unable to clearly communicate what was happening. After getting her to take a few deep breaths and directing her to sit down, she began to pour out what she had been experiencing for the past few hours. She said not long after she had laid down and gone to sleep she woke up to small stones hitting her bedroom window. Thinking some teenagers nearby had decided to pull a late-night stunt she saw nothing moving or any signs of life that could explain the stones hitting her windows. Then she said almost immediately there was a strong malevolent presence in her room coupled with the sensation that the room was closing in upon her. Then she felt as if she was suffocating in the middle of her bed. She tried to pray but couldn't focus. Finally, she cried out to Jesus for help. She said the choking stopped and she then began to sing a hymn and then read a passage of Scripture. But even after a time of singing and reading she said the presence seemed overpowering. She fled the room and moments later appeared at our door totally overwhelmed.

Our ministry experience immediately kicked in and we recognized this for what it was; an attempt by the devil to discourage Kelsey in her spiritual passion and mission pursuit. I suggested we all begin to pray together and we did just that for about thirty minutes or so. Not long after we had started praying the air cleared and we were aware of the Lord's presence once again. Continuing to pray, I asked God to not allow this late-night event to disrupt Kelsey's commitment and purpose in coming to teach in Africa. By the time I closed our prayer time we felt God's unmistakable peace invade the apartment as well as our own hearts. I asked Kelsey to finish her night's rest on the couch in the main room and we would meet for breakfast in a few more hours.

A few days later when we were packing and getting ready to depart Rwanda, we all knew that Kelsey had successfully withstood an attack which would later define her teaching ministry over the next year. Her impact at this particular high school would prove to be immeasurably successful.

In October of 2018, Global Baptist Training Foundation completed its level one of theological training. Except for 2018, it took six years because we had only returned once a year for a total of seven courses. In 2016, we were not able to hold a session because that year there was a state-wide anniversary celebrating reconciliation since the 1994 genocide. We discovered during this time that we had to formulate a plan to cut this time in half or even find a way to finish the first level in two years. Because we had added key classrooms in nearby countries this was made possible by doing back-to-back training sessions in two countries. This is how we are now conducting weekly classrooms throughout the continent. Even now we are beginning to teach two classes per week by lengthening the teaching time per day and holding the graduation on Friday evenings instead of mid-afternoon.

In July of 2018 we were informed by Pastor D that the government had begun an aggressive campaign which demanded that all churches meet certain health and academic standards or else face the possibilities of being closed. The first requirement demanded that proper men's and women's bathrooms be provided in every church operating across the country. This may not sound like a tall order but in many African countries a bathroom consists of a minimalist wooden structure, a door that doesn't shut completely, and once inside, a hole in the floor. Sometimes there is even a roll of toilet paper! The new government standard demanded that all bathrooms be of concrete construction with a concrete hole in the floor or a "high" toilet if available. A "high" toilet is a Western-style toilet. When this mandate was released by the government in January of 2018, there were scores of churches which were prohibited from holding services until they met the standard.

The second standard the government established was that all pastors had to be able to demonstrate that they had been properly trained for their ministry positions. Initially, this appeared to be so subjective it didn't seem possible that a government, much less an inexperienced one, could make reasonable decisions about a local pastor's theological training or establish an appropriate set of standards with a one-size-fits-all mindset. For large numbers of churches and their leaders this posed a significant problem, and had it been six years earlier these Rwandan pastors would have had nothing to suggest any academic or training credentials for their particular ministries. However, from July 2012 to July 2018 this situation was completely changed. It remains to be seen as of this writing exactly how the government will apply established standards to hundreds of churches both in the urban and rural areas of the country, but these pastors who graduated from Global Baptist Training Foundation's level one in October of 2018 are now eager to show officials their earned diplomas in subject areas comparable to any American theological student's resume.

However, these little mission miracles are not the sum total of what God has called us to do. It had became clear to us from the earliest years of teaching and travel back and forth to Africa and East Asia that the job was too big and too broad for a cadre of Western professors. In fact, if it was ever to become just that, we had the growing sense that the foundation's purpose would never be reached. At the beginning of every class I would spend an hour teaching the principles of 2 Tim 2:1-7. I wanted the men and women to know that their knowledge was never to end with them. It became clear to us, even in these early years, that training key national leaders had to be the foremost objective. Unfortunately, until the fall of 2018, no single national trainee appeared to be considering the call to become an official trainer under the guidance of our foundation. That doesn't mean we weren't trying. In every local Asian or African classroom we had singled out the best student pastors to become potential trainers of GBTF materials. These pastors had the best grades, were the most highly motivated, and had stood out as leaders among their peers. We were praying for regional leaders who could effectively train and then eventually replace us.

Finally, in October of 2018, as we began our seventh classroom since 2012, I scheduled some extra time with my translator Fidele on Sunday before our class began on Monday morning. Fidele had been with me for six years and had demonstrated not only a firm grasp of translating English but had also inculcated huge amounts of theological information along the way. If I had a dream pick for the GBTF African training team, Fidele would have been at the top of my list. We had talked on many occasions and he had shared with me the burdens of being a full-time pastor and how his heart was so burdened about evangelism and teaching. He said he never understood why he had these desires while being a pastor but he didn't have any sense of how to change his life trajectory. Then he told me that when GBTF came to Rwanda things began to change. Year by year he told me he became convinced that God was moving him toward fulfilling his real ministry passion. As I sat and listened to him that morning I realized that I was watching one of my prayers being answered right in front of my face! Fidele recounted the fears he felt as he wondered how he would be able to feed his wife and children, provide transportation, or even pay rent somewhere. Despite his reservations about an uncertain future, he then looked across the table and told me that he had officially resigned his church just months earlier. Smiling and confident in his decision, he then said he had surrendered to God to become the first GBTF trainer in East Africa!

As I listened to Fidele that morning I recognized at that moment after six long years: God had given us our first African national trainer. This is exactly what we had dreamed about, talked about, worked for, and prayed for, but now it had finally become a reality.

## The Congo

My former college student, whom I had taught in Boston, and who was responsible for my first Rwandan introduction was actually born in the Congo. He had lived and grown up there before seeking to train for the ministry in New England. There were many colleges he could have sought out for his training but God providentially led him to the one where I had been teaching since 2003. I could never forget this individual because he was always late to class. I'm not talking about sometimes late. That's a different matter. This guy was constantly late, and no matter how often you cajoled him about leaving earlier to fight the Boston traffic, it never changed. Somehow he was able to get past the usual academic disciplines for his bad habit and graduate. In the end, I'm glad he did. He not only became a good student, he went on to be accepted at a Boston seminary for an advanced degree. Furthermore, he was solely responsible for introducing me to the city of Bukavu in southeastern Congo in order to hold a GBTF classroom there in 2012. After closing the Rwanda class on Friday afternoon, he and I boarded one of the local sixteen passenger buses which ran between Kigali and south to the border of the Congo.

In 2012 these buses ran every day to the south border of the Congo several times a day, so we boarded in early afternoon for the six-hour trip. The drivers of these buses were paid according to the number of return trips they would make. All I remember about that first ride was my Congolese student furiously yelling at the driver to slow down. Unfortunately, he never did, but we did make it safely to the border alive and well. I can't say that for all this bus line's riders. This particular bus company averaged about a hundred deaths a year on this route resulting from reckless, high-speed collisions and crashes. I didn't know that fact until after I took my third trip.

For the first three years of the foundation's work in Africa this classroom in Bukavu was held each year in July after the Rwanda classroom. We began in a small church building just outside of the city and for the first two years it averaged about sixty pastors. At the time we were actively engaged in three countries and all of them were what we formerly called Third World. We use the term *developing* these days but the Congo was then and continues to be a nation marked by systemic poverty and desperation. Since the Belgians relinquished control of the country in the early 60s, infrastructure has basically been frozen in time. The street pavement is mostly gone but where it exists there are huge potholes which litter what remains. In Bukavu, many of the dilapidated buildings are exactly how the Belgians left them almost sixty years ago. Although there is some running water in the city and sewer drainage, these simple amenities do not exist. Despite that the Congo has been blessed with innumerable natural resources, the country's citizens do not receive direct benefit from their own country's innate wealth.

One of the greatest examples of this is that the Congo has tremendous hydrological power assets. Unfortunately, much of this raw power in the past has been sold to surrounding nations instead of being used in the maintenance of its own people. Consequently, there are roving power blackouts that plague the populace almost daily. On a few occasions when I was going back to our host's house after dark, I was forced to use my cell phone light to navigate the streets in order to avoid serious injury by either spraining ankles or by falling into holes big enough in which to be buried. I think it was in the Congo where I began to see just what systemic or chronic poverty both looks and feels like. I have had moments in ministry where I felt hopeless, at least as far as defining it as a passing emotion, but in much of the Congo, hopelessness is like a shirt or a pair of shoes that everyone is wearing—every single hour. It wakes up with you every day and lays down with you every night.

The first two years I taught in Bukavu, I taught the first courses of level one which consist of interpretation of Scripture, bibliology, Christology, and anthropology. These basic courses are always well-received and encouraging to the pastors. The third year we focus on soteriology—the study of salvation. It is a rich, fully orbed study which ties together so much of the OT and NT sections that it demands an intense use of the Bible during the entire teaching week. By Wednesday of that third year in 2015, I began to notice that many of the pastors were not participating in the reading of Scriptures which I asked them to read as we covered various parts of the course material.

So just after giving them their take-home quiz for that day's session I asked how many of them did not have a good Bible with them for the class. There were ninety students enrolled, both men and some women, and about seventy of them raised their hands. I was dumbfounded at the sheer number of hands which went up. My follow-up question was what kind of Bibles they had available to them. Half of that number showed me copies of cheap paraphrase Bibles printed in French. Others held up the New World Translation of the Jehovah's Witnesses. I realized then that many of my students from the previous year in Christology had used a translation which teaches that Jesus is a *created being* and not actually *God in the flesh*. I had to hide my tears while I told them I would go home and raise the funds to buy each of them a good study bible in French. They were ecstatic. Once I got home and told my wife we shared this on social media with GBTF followers. We had calculated that we could buy a good study bible for all seventy for right around $400 US. In less than ten days we had $1,400 donated for Bibles in the Congo. We decided to use the remainder for purchasing more Bibles along with Bible commentaries for some of their brethren in West Africa. We sent the money for Congo Bibles to our hosts who then purchased the Bibles in a nearby city, transported them personally to Bukavu, and then distributed them to the pastors and woman students.

When I returned the next year, I was swarmed by those same men and women who couldn't thank us enough for having placed a trustworthy copy of the Scriptures in their hands. I couldn't help but think of how many Bibles most American Christians possess just sitting on their coffee tables or bookshelves, seldom used and perhaps seldom read. None of this is more evident than when you are in a country like the Congo. Everything I take for granted as a Western Christian becomes a source of grateful praise for nearly all of my pastoral students globally, but especially in the DCR.

Unfortunately, as a result of the recent political and social chaos, the Congolese GBTF classrooms have been inactive for the past three years as of this writing, but the future looks bright for renewed activity and training. Our Congolese-born translator-turned-GBTF-trainer, being a native Congolese believer, is deeply burdened about reaching and training leaders in his own country with the gospel. Our hopes of commencing a new classroom are alive and well.

## Liberia

The more I returned to Rwanda and Congo in the early years of the foundation, I could never get away from Annetta's conversation with me after church that day in New England. Like many Liberians in the post-civil-war era, she had immigrated to America hoping for a better life; in fact just the promise of life itself was a blessing. Her descriptions of the country made me wonder why anyone would have stayed. By the time the chaos was over, the war had become a conflict between scores of warring factions who all thought their own acquisition of power would end the war. The danger and uncertainty this generated among the populace was almost unbearable at times. During the most chaotic and dangerous periods the pastor who was to become our GBTF host was playing a significant role in meeting the needs of many of the Liberian pastors struggling to stay alive.

Pastor J was a well known Baptist pastor and evangelical leader for twenty-five years prior to the civil wars. Once the second war had begun Pastor J moved his family into Ghana for safe keeping. During the height of the war, factional groups both in the cities and in the rural areas would stop vehicles anywhere they found them. If they didn't like your answers or you didn't appear to be on their side, they would often kill you on the spot or send you to a location where you would be dispatched out of public view. Once a month he would cross back over the border and covertly travel the backroads trying to meet the needs of pastors and their families who were trying to keep their congregations together in the midst of the chaos.

On one of those clandestine excursions he was stopped just outside of Monrovia by some enforcers of a particular faction. After a brief explanation and without warning they sent him with four men to one of their death houses. He told me that without intervention that day, his life would have ended within an hour or so. At one of the government-held roads was a vehicle checkpoint they had to pass through before reaching the house. Pastor J was sitting between two men in the back seat when, for no apparent reason, the guard outside told the driver to tell the man in the middle of the back seat to exit the car. When he did, he motioned the car on without him. Pastor J told me he didn't know who his benefactor was or why the guard had told his captors to release him, and he has never seen him again to thank him for it.

When the war ended in 2003 Pastor J moved his family back into the capital of Monrovia. While many, like our church member Annetta, were fleeing the war-torn nation, Pastor J began once again to pour into the churches and pastors who had survived.

Pastor J, among other Christian evangelicals, was fighting an uphill spiritual battle. Between 1980 and 1990 Libya's Moammar Gaddaffi invested up to $100 million US in the country in order to make it a potential satellite partner with the Libyan regime in Libya. In the effort to build collaboration Gaddaffi, along with the assistance of Saudi Arabia, who also wanted to consolidate political power, financed the building of a mosque in every reasonably sized town. On the way to our classroom from the capital of Monrovia to Gbarnga in Bong County, small mosques can be seen all along the way in village after village. Many of them, hardly used, were built in the hope that the Islamization of Liberia would be imminent in the post-civil-war era. Their efforts continue but without the grandiose results for which they had hoped.

In 2015, Pastor J heard about the efforts of GBTF to train pastors. One of the Rwandan or Congolese students from an earlier class had shared some pictures over the internet. In late 2016, Pastor J reached out by email to the foundation requesting a classroom. We receive requests like this fairly regularly and upon every invitation to come is a vetting process. As you can imagine, this process is not easy for any of us. Our objective in vetting potential hosts is to make sure the request is being made in good faith. There is a powerful desire among the indigenous to better their lives.

Unfortunately, many native Africans have been deprived through systemic poverty and corruption for so long, they have unwittingly been infected with some form of the disease. Christianity offers the greatest antidote to this moral crisis, but even then, trusting God alone for one's needs is not just a Third World problem. What makes it so difficult in developing countries is that chronic *dependence* has been produced by a host of issues embedded deep in the culture. Secondly, the corruption of the political system guarantees the infection will eventually run from the top of the head to the sole of the foot. Both help support the false perception that Americans are just as systemically rich as the indigenous are poor. Consequently it becomes very easy when working with them for costs to be ignored or undervalued.

For instance, our foundation provides a noon meal for the pastors each of the five days of class. We discovered early on that you cannot teach a hungry pastor. The number of pastors we feed is also critically important in determining overall meal expense. We attempt to become knowledgable about the local costs of rice, beans, bagged or bottled water, and the necessary amenities so we don't unnecessarily overpay or force our host to incur expenses they can't afford to cover.

One of the primary tasks of vetting a potential host is being able to determine if the inquiring host shares the values of both integrity and hard work with the foundation as we offer them free training delivered in person to their front door. This of course sounds much easier than it actually works out to be. In much of the developing world, the populace, through no fault of their own, have at times had to depend on the United Nations, disaster relief organizations, and even good old American grants to their nation in order for people to survive. When GBTF shows up to provide quality theological training without cost we realize that there can still be a question of what else we might be willing to provide. Again, we don't blame either our hosts or our students for that perception. However, starting on the first day of class we choose to emphasize some key spiritual truths with pastors that we believe must be embraced in order for the ultimate mission of training leaders to take place.

First, we emphasize the need for them to reproduce their training in others. They are given a fully developed syllabus in their native tongue so they can immediately begin teaching their churches the same material they have been taught. Many native pastors have to be convinced that they are capable of training others. I always tell them they can always teach what they know, but they can never teach what they haven't learned. And, as we all know, you learn more through teaching than you do as a student. Secondly, we begin immediately to look out for the most capable students who can become national leaders who train other pastors. This component insures a future at some point without the aid of GBTF. I tell them I love them but the day may arrive when returning for another classroom may become impossible. The goal is that they become independent trainers in their own countries.

We started the Liberian classroom in January of 2017. Pastor J met me at the airport about 2 AM on a Sunday morning. We drove through the night down toward Bong County from the capital. We passed the backroads through miles of rubber trees belonging to the Firestone company. The majority of Firestone tires originate right here among the hundreds of acres of the Firestone rubber tree groves. Around six in the morning we arrived in Gbarnga where the Baptist Health clinic and camp are located where this classroom has met for nearly three years. Pastor J drove me right over to a local hotel where he had reserved a room a month earlier. When we pulled up to the location I noticed several UN vehicles parked outside. In the developing world of Africa, the UN wields an unusual level of both influence and power among the populace. This becomes noticeable in the way their workers act and expect to be treated. You get the impression that they exist in another world on the continent.

When Pastor J and I went into the hotel to get me settled for the rest of the day and night, the sub-manager told us the room was no longer available. After he told us that the UN had come in and claimed every room for the week at twice the normal price we needed no further explanation. Pastor J was visibly angry with the owner but he was conveniently nowhere to be found, so we were forced to take a room at another hotel about a half-mile away at about half the quality. Neither one was Disneyland, but this one had no showers and was equipped with just a fifty-gallon drum of fresh water and a bucket in the bathroom for personal bathing. That is accompanied of course by the reality of cold water only, but in this part of world, clean water for bathing is preferable to none at all, and it can really boost your morale after a long, hot teaching day.

Pastor J picked me up early Monday morning and we headed over to the classroom at the health center. When we arrived it was gratifying to see a large group of pastors standing and talking eagerly waiting for the teacher to arrive. After a few minutes of Pastor

J giving instructions to a few of the men from the truck window, he got out and unloaded several boxes. One of them was loaded with freshly printed t-shirts with the GBTF logo in front and the date of the week's classroom emblazoned on the back. They were kind of a golden yellow so that morning I happily taught a group of even happier pastors proudly donning their new shirts. The picture of that first Liberian classroom's graduates in a sea of yellow hangs proudly on our GBTF office wall. Even without the help of the shirts the Liberian pastors seemed to share a solidarity unlike any of the other African nations. I'm not sure exactly why but the effects of fifteen years of civil war must play a key role.

In the first class in 2017 we had sixty-two pastors who came from all over the country for training. Usually in the first classroom in any new location there are pockets of pastors who wait to see how that first class goes in order to determine their participation in future classes. In this case, the majority of area pastors rallied to be involved in that first classroom. Liberia has also been the first African country to benefit from GBTF holding two classes per year in each location. This expedites the training and allows pastors to finish the seven courses in level one in less than three years. This quickened pace of training then allows us to discover and prepare national trainers much faster. It's our hope that the first Liberian trainer(s) will come forward before completing level one.

Despite the fact that there has been a good turnout of pastors in Bong County there remain scores of pastors in the capital of Monrovia and in the outer perimeters of the country who are requesting classrooms in addition to what GBTF is presently doing. This is a very encouraging sign because there has already been over one hundred new church plants in under two years resultant from GBTF pastoral students. We are asking God to allow GBTF pastors to begin five hundred new churches in three more years. As many as half of this group will come from Bong County students alone. The church planting possibilities coming from trained men in the capital and the outbound areas will likely surpass that number once classrooms are initiated there.

Once again, I think it's important to be reminded that this kind of output is simply unheard of in most scenarios where Western missionary families are involved. Necessarily, there is no fault to be found with the missionaries themselves. It may be that if the mission work is among unreached people groups the progress may remain slow for several years. We have to account for the translation of the Scriptures into the host language, the reaching of individuals who can be successfully trained for leadership, and other long-term goals unique to reaching into virgin areas with the gospel of Christ.

However, if these obstacles are not present, the nationals themselves are the best and most productive means possible to move and multiply the gospel forward. We will talk more about this in a later chapter.

## Togo

We began the training of Togolese national pastors in January of 2016. This little West African country has a long history going back several centuries but in the nineteenth century it earned the nickname "The Slave Coast." After WWI the country was divided among the British and the French. When WWII ended the British voted to move their allegiance to Ghana and by1960 the UN ceded control of the entire country of Togo to the French.

Pastor S emailed our office late in 2015 and asked us to consider holding a classroom in Lome, the capital. Because this was our first invitation from West Africa we gave immediate consideration to the request, despite the fact that we had no funding available to open another class. We prayed, and while we sought God's leadership we sent the appropriate questionnaires to Pastor S along with the written expectations for any country-wide national host. After a month or so of deliberation and prayer our board moved ahead and we added Togo to our list of active classrooms.

Our first three Togolese classrooms were held at an older American Baptist seminary in the capital city which is now owned by the Southern Baptists but the institution is only able to train a small contingent of pastors who are able to afford the costs of education. Despite the fact that the seminary is heavily subsidized by the SBC, the vast majority of the pastors with whom we interact are not able to squeeze anything out of their meager incomes for education. Consequently, during the week we held a class the seminary was a beehive of activity and excitement with GBTF students coming and going each morning and afternoon. We have averaged right around fifty to sixty-five pastors over the past three years, and even though we have moved on from the seminary, the determination among the pastors remains constant. One of the issues we have faced with this class, not unlike other unstable countries in which we operate, has been political unrest. One of our planned classrooms had to be canceled because of violence in the capital. Our host has also suffered from personal violence on the streets around the area where he lives, and just recently had armed robbers enter his home. We have asked our foundation supporters and social media followers to pray for Pastor S and his family on several occasions.

One of the other realities which our hosts face in Togo and one which we have become increasingly familiar is demon activity. This is an uncomfortable subject with most American Christians but is very commonplace, particularly in Africa. One year Pastor S drove us out of the capital to some of the villages beyond the city limits. He had been praying for several of them and wanted me to see them for myself. I noticed that nearly all of them had flags raised at the entrance gate of the village. I asked him what the flags represented. He said the flags represented the spiritual focus of the entire village and often they identified themselves as worshippers of either animistic deities or were openly satanic. Pastor S identified one of them to me as a village of devil worshippers and one in which he was attempting to influence but in order to do this he would have to develop a relationship with the village chief. Although this seems formidable, if the chief can be won to Christ, the village itself would likely follow him.

My translator in Togo is Pastor D (not the same Pastor D from Rwanda) and he lives and ministers in the northern area of the country where demonism abounds. One of the common practices found here is what is called astral projection. In the West we were introduced to this practice with the influx of Eastern religious practices back in the 60s and 70s. Under the influence of mind-altering drugs, practitioners would apparently leave their own bodies and travel indefinite distances to specific locations which they would later describe in detail once they had returned to their bodies and normal state of mind. In Togo, this is practiced without the aid of drugs.

One day a few years ago I was having a conversation with Pastor D about his experiences with demonism where he and his family live in the north. He told me one evening before dusk in his small town he was standing at a street corner where there were a lot of people standing, talking, or buying odds and ends from locals, mostly home-made foodstuffs to take home for feeding families. All of the sudden he said out of the sky dropped two naked bodies onto the pavement. I said, "What do you mean dropped out of the sky?" I wanted to make sure he wasn't talking about people jumping out of trees, or off buildings. He simply shook his head and reiterated that they came directly out of the sky itself. I was incredulous and forced him to provide further details which would somehow make sense to my Western senses of scientific order. I finally blurted out "Where did they come from?" His reply was that he wasn't exactly sure but he believed that demon entities may have come and stolen the bodies of those practicing astral projection before they had time to return to them. I then asked him if the bodies that dropped out of the sky had been injured or killed by the fall. He said they ran off and he didn't know what became of them. Having seen enough of demonism myself for the past several years I questioned him no further and realized that further questioning would be fruitless.

On another occasion our host had taken my wife and I to a local eating spot. When we exited the car we noticed a couple of village women beating grain in a large wooden bowl with a fencepost-sized pestal. We decided we would take a picture of the women and as we lined up the shot the two women took notice of me taking their picture. I can't describe for you the look in the eyes of these women but as the saying goes, if looks could kill, we would still be in Africa, and I'm talking about more than a few ladies who didn't care to have their picture taken. We were both momentarily concerned with a physical altercation, but fortunately for our sake they settled down and we were able to go sit down and have our meal.

Togo provides a significant West African challenge to GBTF as we continue to see God raise up pastors who want to duplicate their training in other leaders. If the past is a precursor to the future, Togo may hold the greatest potential for multiplying the gospel forward in the other French-speaking nations of West Africa such as Senegal, Mali, Guinea, Mauritania, Cote d'Ivoire, Burkina Faso, and Benin.

## Haiti

In 2015 a group of churches in North Carolina asked me to train the Haitian pastors associated with their Haitian orphanage ministry under the direction of a native Haitian. This national pastor had narrowly survived the major earthquake which struck in 2010. He was in a government building on January 12 when the earthquake occurred. The building collapsed, killing scores of people inside. When the shaking stopped he found himself standing at the end of the building floors which had remained intact. The remainder of the building was completely demolished. He and one other man beside him survived that day. There were no others who made it out alive. He immediately climbed out from the rubble and made his way from town to his orphanage to find that God had graciously spared all of his children.

While in North Carolina we met with the Haitian native, Pastor C. Since we had recently screened another Haitian pastor for holding a classroom the following month I asked Pastor C to join me to monitor the class so he would be able to make a wise decision about hosting a classroom sometime later the next year, which he did in the spring of 2016. That class had about FIFTY pastors present along a coastal area southwest of the capital. Unfortunately, because Pastor C and the North Carolina board have ceased joint ministries we have not been able to return to that area.

However, while teaching in Boston before the start of Global Baptist Training Foundation, I had a colleague who also served as an adjunct on staff at our college. He had been invited to teach in Haiti after earning his doctorate in 2010 and had made several strong contacts in Port aux Prince, the capital. Once we began the foundation my friend asked me about teaching a class in the capital with him in the spring of 2016. Since then we have scheduled two other GBTF classrooms and taught these classes together. Unfortunately, the last two classes we have scheduled have been canceled due to political violence in the capital. Normally we don't cancel classes easily. We usually depend on our host's judgement on whether or not a classroom is viable. We will also check with the local US embassy on day-to-day conditions and take recommendations from their offices. On our latest canceled classroom the embassy had removed all non-essential government workers. This is always a good sign to cancel a class, especially in the capital city of Port aux Prince. Whenever there is violence in Haiti it is always the most intense in the capital city. If you cannot make it safely from the airport to your host's home or hotel, there is no need to buy a plane ticket.

We take this part of the Lord's work very seriously but we will not place a professor or local host in danger unnecessarily. In many parts of the world today, Westerners can be easily spotted and targeted for violence so this is a constant concern from the time we land until the time we fly back out.

Haiti remains and will continue to be a focus of the training we offer indigenous spiritual leaders. The political and spiritual corruption in the country cannot be measured by any reliable standard. The degradation of the country has been ongoing for decades and without a major shift in the forces which control the country in both the spiritual and political realms Haiti simply has no hope for a brighter future. Our commitment to train local church leaders offers the most significant possibilities for fostering change and renewal, but there is more. Beyond the training of pastors under his local leadership, Pastor C is also getting training at the best college of political science in Port aux Prince, and prays daily that God will open a door for him into Haiti's political world. Pastor C will need all of our prayers to achieve such a goal.

## Myanmar

One of the best Christian biographies I ever read was about the first American missionary to leave American shores in 1812 bound for India. His name was Adoniram Judson and this brilliant young man had just asked and received permission for the hand in marriage of a daughter of a local pastor in Malden, Massachusetts. This took place just a month before they had set sail. Now married for two weeks, they embarked on a voyage for the East from which this Congregational pastor's daughter would never return. Her name was Anne Hasselltine Judson and their story is best told in the book by Courtney Anderson entitled *To the Golden Shore*. When I was very young in my ministry my wife and I read it every year for five or six years while we were in a challenging Canadian church planting ministry. There was simply no way to stay discouraged in the Lord's work after reading the Judson's story.

When we began GBTF I wondered if God would ever open the door to training nationals in Myanmar. I knew of some American pastors who had contact with some national pastors there but I had no idea how to make meaningful contact with them. One day in February of 2012, a pastor walked into my office and introduced me proudly to a visiting Myanmar national pastor who had heard about the beginning of GBTF. We had literally been in operation no more than three months and barely had a website created and functioning. When Pastor V reached out and shook my hand his first words were if I would be willing to come to the capital of Yangon and train twenty-five to thirty pastors at his church later that year. I was so ecstatic I think he had to repeat the question!

In October of 2012 we were able to hold our first classroom in the land of Judson, the American missionary who was the first to give them the gospel, their first Christian churches, a Burmese translation of the Scriptures, and a Bible dictionary. Pastor V himself was a fifth-generation convert of Judson. We held the class outside in a makeshift room with bamboo curtain walls and goats and chickens all around the area. During one afternoon class a baby goat sauntered through the classroom and back out the other end. I have had chickens, dogs, and a host of other students who have stopped by for training on occasion as well! On Friday one of my students whose own dad (Pastor M) pastored across town invited us to come and meet him and his congregation. I spent the afternoon teaching a large group of young men and women a short section of one of Paul's epistles. In later years we have taught for Pastor M yearly.

While in our third classroom in Yangon with Pastor V, his dad sat in on the class. He was also a pastor who led a church north of Yangon. At the end of the week he asked us to hold a classroom with his church and the area pastors. I had never heard of the town but there were a couple of larger cities nearby with which I was familiar. We scheduled a class for the following year and for the first time scheduled multiple classes. When I got home from that classroom my wife picked me up at the airport and was excited to tell me about having met a young man at our grocery store from Myanmar.

So early the next week we went shopping and I had the privilege of meeting Sing. Sing had a small sushi counter in the seafood department and was busy when we made our way to his counter. He seemed very happy to meet me and we instantly began talking about his home country. It wasn't long before Sing began visiting our home for meals and family gatherings. We basically adopted him into the family. I asked Sing early on about his spiritual life. He said he wasn't a Buddhist like most people from Myanmar but that he was Christian. I knew that this didn't mean Sing was a professing believer in Jesus but only a Christian by name. I encouraged him to read his Bible and also spent time sharing my faith with him. He told us that his parents had prayed that God would lead him to a strong Christian family once he arrived in Florida. We said congratulations God has answered your parent's prayers. Sing knew that was true and was visibly humbled by that fact, but all we could do was pray for him to come to Christ. Our other married kids in town did the same and Sing would show his appreciation for our family's love by holding sushi parties at one of their homes. It was great fun and Sing greatly enjoyed having a local family.

Not long from the time we met, Sing got in a serious car accident and nearly lost his life. God spared him and when Sing became ambulatory once again we invited him for dinner. When he sat down in our home I asked him why he thought God had allowed him to live. He said because you and my parents were praying for me to know Jesus. I said, "Yes you are right. I hope that you will soon know Him."

Not many days after that night Sing sat in our home and confessed that he had bowed his heart to the Savior and now knew the difference between calling oneself a Christian and really being one. We rejoiced with him that evening and encouraged him to call his parents with the news of his salvation. Later that year Sing invited my wife and I out for dinner and during the meal I told him about the plan to teach three classes that year back-to-back; two in Yangon, and the third in a small village in the north at the foothills of the mountains. Sing casually asked me the name of the town and just as casually I said the name of the town was *Ka-lem-yo.* The word wasn't barely out of my mouth when Sing's eyes grew wide and then he just sat there like he didn't know what to say next. Then he blurted out "That's my village!" For a moment we all just sat there stunned, because who could have known that the plan to teach in Kalemyo several months earlier would end up being the hometown of our recently born-again sushi boy at our local grocery store? Only God can arrange stuff like that! The amazing thing about it all was the fact that I would now have the privilege of looking into the faces of his sisters and mom and dad for the first time and confirm for them what Sing had already told them on the phone.

Just a few months later I boarded a plane for East Asia with my carry-on bag loaded to the gills with gifts for his parents and siblings. After my host met me at the airport and took me to my hotel, Sing's parents came to meet me. It was a joyous occasion and one I will never forget.

The classroom went well and on Thursday of that week, his parents invited me to their home for dinner. They cooked several local dishes and wanted to somehow convey to me their love and appreciation for impacting their son and being the answer to their years of prayer that he would find Christ somewhere along his way. They were telling me all this through a translator eating at the table with us when all of a sudden Sing's dad said something else that both stunned and humbled me almost simultaneously. Sing's dad looked at me across the table and said, "You his father now." Although taken aback momentarily, I think I knew that this meant since he could not be there to lead his son further he was handing me the ball and putting me in charge of that responsibility. He was in fact giving me something very valuable to him which he could give only once and to no other. I can still hear the words in my ears to this day.

Last year we held our sixth class in Myanmar, the last three have been among the *Tedim* Chin people from the mountains near the India border. When we returned to the US I had a meeting scheduled in Indianapolis and while there took time to visit the largest Chin congregation in the country which runs around three thousand members from the Hakka Chin dialect. I requested of the pastoral team the opportunity to share our ministry with the congregation in order to encourage their support in reaching the country by training national pastors. We followed that visit up with a letter a month or so later and have not heard anything from them or their central leadership.

We have since learned that even though the Hakka Chin have reached nearly their entire ethnic group, they do not have a significant burden about reaching the rest of the ethnic clans with the gospel. We continue to work in the training of these men and pray that God would use them to reach the nation of Myanmar, which is at present nearly 89 percent Buddhist.

## Mexico

Our ministry in the western hemisphere has been deliberately delayed for several years. We felt that the foundation's initial focus needed to be in Africa and areas around what is known as the 10/40 window. Two-thirds of the world's population—more than 4.4 billion people—live in the 10/40 window. Ninety percent of the people living in the 10/40 window are unevangelized. Many have never heard the gospel message even once. There are either no Christians or not enough Christians in many cultures of the 10/40 window to carry out effective evangelism.

This is not the case in this hemisphere. Mexico and Central America have been effectively evangelized for decades and now have numbers of evangelically minded believers. In many of the rural areas of the country the pastors do not have the opportunity to get education or the money to pay for it; usually it's both. Our introduction to Mexico came from an unlikely but welcome source. An old acquaintance from Bible college retired from the pastorate and wanted to make a difference by helping to establish new church plants worldwide. He heard about what we were doing at GBTF and contacted me about our organizations working in conjunction with each other in areas where we were already training nationals. Since that first meeting we have traveled together, primarily to Africa, allowing him to fund pastors we were training to start new churches. It has been a highly successful relationship and one which will be duplicated globally.

My partner's church planting ministry started in Mexico where he had worked with national pastors in the southern part of the country to replicate churches into the interior, along the coast, and in the mountainous areas. The nationals with whom he has worked are not able to get training mostly because it is only in the bigger cities where seminaries and Bible colleges can be maintained. When they heard that we were working together in Africa many of their leaders asked us to come and offer training. Our first class in Ouxaca was planned and held in September of 2018. We had a modest group of twenty-five and taught the initial course of hermeneutics (interpretation of Scripture) to these student pastors.

In 2019, we will attempt to hold two more classes along the coast as well as for pastors in the mountainous regions. We believe that Mexico holds the key for training scores of nationals not only in Mexico but in Central and South America. The country is strategically placed between geographical areas of extreme unrest and poverty to the south and the US on the northern boundary. Many of those who come looking for better economic prospects will either come through Mexico or remain there for indefinite periods of time. This provides rich opportunities for theological training through Mexican nationals. The language barriers in this part of the world are much less daunting than some. Portugese is the most widely used language, primarily in Brazil, with Spanish coming in a very close second on the continent. This allows for a much less hindered communication system of printed materials and less demand for translators which can speed up the training process. The importance of Mexico cannot be underestimated in the importance of training nationals who can impact the entire continent of South America.

## Uganda

In January of 2018, I taught our fourth classroom in Liberia and our church planting specialist and I took an intra-Africa flight into Entebbe, Uganda, to attend a conference of pastors. From Monrovia to Entebbe that amounts to about three thousand miles and nearly a six-hour flight. We were invited to the conference by an American missionary, Pastor R, in an effort to begin a possible classroom in Entebbe the following July. We landed in Entebbe and drove early the next day to attend the National Independent Baptist Revival Conference being held in Mbarara, a town in southwestern Uganda. Mbarara is about a six-hour drive from Entebbe.

Our driver, Pastor D, is the son of an American missionary and has been in Uganda for twenty-five years. He is the first American missionary we have personally connected with in order to set up a classroom anywhere GBTF presently operates. This is a stunning fact when you consider my original plans for the foundation. Initially, we believed that access to larger numbers of indigenous pastors would have to be done through direct contact with Western missionaries. I reasoned that nationals would have no idea how to make contact unless we initiated it ourselves or relied on American sources. I simply could not have been more uninformed. All the way back to our first official classroom in Yangon, Myanmar, the foundation was immediately contacted by national pastors in India and Pakistan within a month of holding that first classroom. Not only was the original plan totally unnecessary, it was entirely out of touch.

After a night's rest at a small hotel beside the local church, we were given two speaking slots over the next two days to introduce the foundation to the pastors to determine the interest levels for on-site theological training. Excited by the prospects of receiving local training without a bill attached was a huge drawing card for all of the attending pastors. On our last day with the men Pastor D announced to all of them that we would begin praying about holding a class the following October in Entebbe. We didn't realize it at the time but our decision to pray over the real possibility of holding a Ugandan classroom caused Pastor D to take a step of faith himself. On his two-and-a-half-acre property stands an old barn that he wanted to renovate in order to house future training classes. Our decision to seriously pray about adding this African classroom was all the incentive he needed to begin raising money for the project.

In just over one month, before the October 2018 classroom, the building was entirely knocked down, rebuilt, and equipped with forty beds, two large bathrooms, and two private sleeping quarters on each end of the building. The building was nearly at full capacity for our first classroom. We expect that the subsequent classrooms will create demand for even greater ingenuity at housing more pastors who received favorable news of the initial conference.

Since Uganda, known as *the heart of Africa*, is so central to the continent, we believe the growth of this classroom and its influence will open doors into Kenya, Nairobi, and Tanzania, including Malawi and Zambia to the south. With the addition of Fidele, our first African trainer, we fully expect these nations to be participating by holding local classrooms in the next three to five years, if not sooner.

CHAPTER 6

# Balancing Your Missions Plan

## Assessing Your Church's Missions Culture

IF WE ARE TRULY going to change the way we understand and execute our mission plan we have got be willing to see where we are presently using our mission dollars, and then be willing to introduce any necessary changes. I would propose an assessment of what we are doing in terms of *sending* missionary families as well as *training and supporting* indigenous missions on the ground in any country in which we are presently engaged. This is not going to be easy, so if you are looking for a quick fix, it might be a good idea to stop reading here. We have discovered that the vast majority of churches identify with a missions philosophy which relies more on sending missionaries to a location to start churches than it does on utilizing nationals in the same country to do the same kind of ministry.

Why would we feel it is more advantageous to send an English-speaking Western couple, who likely are racially and ethnically different than their target country? Probably because that is how missions has normally been understood and practiced. Now of course, if that is the only solution to advancing the gospel, we have no choice. But what if there are nationals in the country who are evangelically minded believers who can be contacted, trained, and then sent out locally? These individuals already know the language of the people, understand the culture, and have a native burden to reach them with the gospel message. That is a much better and a more effective solution in moving and multiplying the gospel forward when possible. This latter scenario is precisely what Global Baptist Training Foundation has had the privilege of doing for nearly seven years.

## Finding the Balancing Point

Every missions pastor has to come to grips with how the church missions program is designed. That sweet spot of balancing funding between missionaries who are taking the gospel to geographically unreached people groups versus funding indigenous pastors who actively train others must be found. Finding that balancing point is important because in many cases, evangelizing unreached people groups may be better done by those who are geographically, racially, ethnically, and culturally nearer to the target audience.

For example, I have an acquaintance who trains pastors in the Eastern Bloc. He has a real burden for reaching into Russia with the gospel but cannot do so legally. Consequently, he has for several years trained Ukrainian pastors to both reach and train Russians for Christ. They are both equipped and capable of crossing the border to advance the gospel in the former Soviet Union more effectively than anyone. Yes, oftentimes, they have to do this underground but they are much less prone to being suspected or arrested because they speak the language, blend into the culture, and deeply care about the people.

Since the Orthodox Russian Church, which is closely aligned to the Soviet government, is the only *legal* religious group under the current Putin regime, evangelization has to be done underground. In this case, empowering nationals is the only way to advance the gospel here. Other Communist nations like North Korea, Cuba, and China must be reached by nationals in a similar way.

## What About the Status Quo?

I have often heard pastors and missionaries talk about all that they *didn't* learn in seminary or Bible college. There are parallels in nearly every profession imaginable. The doctor is trained in his or her speciality but once they are outside that discipline in the area of *preventative* medicine, they are often like a ship out of water.

On one occasion I contracted a fairly normal case of intestinal parasites resulting from not following protocol while traveling last year and once I was diagnosed, I was prescribed a powerful antibiotic. Unfortunately, I was not given much else to do and just after finishing the round of antibiotics I happened to have a conversation with someone who had experienced a similar issue who told me about the need to prevent future infestations resulting from eggs existing in the intestinal tract. I wasn't told that the real problem is in eradicating all the eggs that can eventually re-hatch in your system after killing the initial parasites. I immediately began a second round of naturopathic treatments which eventually eradicated the problem for good, but it would have been better if I had been more informed from the beginning. This couldn't be more true than in the ministry. We seem to encounter all the problems in ministry that we learned nothing about in our training.

It wasn't long after I resigned my teaching and church leadership positions that I saw the magnitude of our endeavor. My own pastor reiterated this to me in some of our initial meetings. The economy was in a trough of despair and this was being reflected in many other churches. We both agreed that not only was this new 501(c)(3) foundation going to be a big step of faith, it was going to be difficult. If I hadn't known tough ministry experiences previously, it is likely this venture would have been overwhelming. However, like shepherd David's confident reminder to King Saul in the face of Goliath that he had previously knocked off both a lion and a bear, we too were confident that God's calling was going to become his enablement. It was.

Despite the fact our board voted that the foundation would pay a small salary from the time we started, we decided that we would do everything, with the exception of a housing allowance, to manage our own expenses so the ministry itself could grow. We have never regretted that decision. There may come a time when we will accept a salary but that time is still in the foreseeable future. In the first thirty-six to forty-eight months after our job resignations, I spent weekends presenting the ministry of training nationals in every church that would have us. We were able to gather support from several churches on the same level that regular missionaries are normally supported monthly, mostly from those who knew me from teaching at a regional Bible college. There were some exceptions but this was the pattern we saw developing. But unfortunately, as we received invitations to hold classrooms in Asia and Africa, we learned that we had to raise significant funding outside of local church support to be able to conduct the actual ministry. We couldn't raise enough support from churches we knew to be able to regularly buy international air travel along with the expenses related to translation, classroom costs, as well as personal maintenance for up to two weeks in the Third World.

In the process of coming to understand this I began to call hundreds of churches. Normally this involves talking with a person in the office, leaving a message for the missions pastor or senior pastor, and then hoping for a return call. Probably 50 percent of calls I made began and ended right there with the person in the office. The distinct impression made was that the person was being protected from all callers except those that constituted an actual emergency, whatever that might be. I can count on one hand how many times I was patched into a primary leader's office for a direct conversation. If I was, it was almost always to leave a voicemail which would nearly never be returned. During one week, a hundred calls were made and I did not receive one response from a missions director or senior pastor. Fortunately, having been a senior pastor for many years I was not unaware of the number of calls any reasonably busy pastor is subject to each day. Without a screening process, a pastor could ostensibly spend half his waking hours taking calls.

There are perhaps many reasons for this lack of response, and I believe that is the best word to use: *response*. No *response* is perhaps the *easiest* way for an overburdened pastor with an over-burdened ministry budget to answer those who are seeking to add still more burden and more weight to his portfolio. Just how often can a leader explain to those looking to him for assistance that the church simply can't add any more responsibility at this time, without becoming discouraged himself? Can you blame him? Yes, I know there may be better solutions than choosing not to respond, but it's important to understand that part of the issue. Most of us would rather die from anything than a thousand little cuts.

But this raises the larger question: How can a missionary or anyone who does ministry in conjunction with other local churches get a hearing for what God is doing in their life and ministry? What needs to change? This is likely one of the most profound questions for churches, local church-based organizations like ours, and missionaries who require support to fulfill their mission. The church landscape has drastically changed in the last twenty-five years.

The majority of evangelically minded churches have historically held at least two all-church meetings each week. In most Baptist circles this much was true because in many of the independent churches a Sunday night service was part of the service schedule for well over a century. This schedule usually included a mid-week meeting as well. That service schedule is no longer being practiced by the majority of churches today.

In many cases, there are still as many as two services a week held in the church facility but only one of those involves the entire body meeting together, and that is usually in two to three separate Sunday morning services. For independent churches this greatly curtails the amount of time a church has dedicated solely to worship. Any pastor is going to be very reticent about turning over his preaching time to anyone, unless it directly connects to his worship schedule in some meaningful way. Others may give a three- to five-minute time slot to share with the congregation what they are doing in the field, but it offers little opportunity to mission families who are just starting out raising support. The consequences of this are predictable. The average time for an independent missionary family to reach their God-called ministry field can be as much as three to five years when raising their own support. There are many variations of that number, but at the same time this has forced missionaries to not just rely on churches as the sole means of their own mission support.

Social media is now a significant part of the equation which offers them contact with followers of their ministry through their own blog sites, mission website, or personal Facebook, Twitter, and Instagram accounts. Even though the social media providers are constantly morphing and changing practices, social media now allows those with viable ministry needs to get them out into public view to raise additional support from friends and followers. This has changed the dynamic for many missionaries as well as churches who support them.

Most local church missionaries are approved and sent out by a home church or mission board. These organizations can act as 501(c)(3) non-profits and provide the means necessary to receive and account for donations given to a single missionary family or mission. They send out tax receipts to donors and handle other important paper work. Money that is raised online or through any private website for ministry would not necessarily be able to furnish a tax receipt. Hopefully, this would not keep any donor from giving toward a worthy cause but unfortunately it does. Many donors equate credibility with the accountability an official 501(c)(3) provides, and you cannot remain in operation for long if your books don't add up correctly. History demonstrates that it takes a lot more effort to run an organization with a deliberate *lack* of integrity than otherwise.

For missionaries sent through the Southern Baptist Convention very few of the above concerns apply. All missions giving is done through the Cooperative Program's administrative agencies. Those who are supported through the International Mission Board are fully supported from the time they are approved by the board. This allows them the breathing room to focus on ministry essentials without the concerns that finances can bring. It also means that all of the travel and face time with churches is eliminated.

Even with the changing face of available service times this barely affects the average Southern Baptist Convention missionary. This is also a great savings of energy and resources in the life of the missionaries themselves. It also allows them to begin their ministries immediately upon their approval through the SBC administrative arms. So is that all? Not really.

One of the biggest complaints of the average SBC church member is their lack of contact with the missionaries they support through their local churches. SBC missionaries are supported with a percentage of undesignated giving receipts coupled with the two big missions offerings taken yearly in every SBC church; the Lottie Moon Christmas offering and the Annie Armstrong Easter offering. Because the missionaries are supported immediately upon approval, the vast majority of SBC donors among their 46,000 churches seldom meet or get an opportunity to interact with the missionaries they support through the IMB and ultimately, their local churches. It's very difficult to know what level of impact this has upon real giving but this lack of personal knowledge and interaction cannot enhance giving at the pew level. However, unable to prove either a negative or the effects of a negative, we can only speculate on what the SBC could raise through the Cooperative Program above present levels otherwise. However, there are exceptions.

Because our home church is in another state, my wife and I, when not traveling, attend an SBC church in our city. We both love great music and crave solid preaching and teaching when available. This church has both and often has furloughed, or new missionaries appear on the platform on Sunday mornings for a quick interview by the senior pastor. It is effective and always concludes with a encouragement by the pastor to meet with this missionary after the service. This is the kind of face-time that helps people keep missions front and center in Christian service. Most people want a hands-on kind of experience in ministry today and this is especially true in how they invest their financial resources in advancing the gospel globally. Whether you operate your ministry as an independent or within a convention of churches, operational integrity must remain the key to generating trust and growth.

## What Do the Nationals Say?

This question is likely the most relevant question for all of us interested in the spreading of the gospel of Jesus Christ. After all, our job is to train faithful men who will reach their populaces. The only real question after that is deciding who is best qualified to do that. Initially, among any unreached people group, outsiders must be directed by God to go to initiate the process of evangelism and church planting. Other scenarios involve unreached geographical areas within countries already evangelized to some degree, and sending trained individuals from within the country to reach specific areas. This should be the starting point from where we should answer the question "What do the Nationals Say?" In fact, I ask this question in every nation where GBTF is presently training the indigenous. The answers vary from country to country but the reality is the same everywhere.

Nationals instinctively know that they are better equipped to reach their own people than anyone else. Why shouldn't they? They know the native tongue and use it more effectively than any foreigner likely ever could in a lifetime. They are much more likely to understand dialectical oddities and would be capable of moving comfortably into regional dialects as a situation demanded it. This enables both spontaneous conversation and translates into much less strained communication, especially when it involves the gospel of Christ. Western missionaries will often confess that the greatest hurdle to missionary life is mastering the host language, and this takes several years of technical learning and then practical application.

Whenever GBTF opens a new class anywhere in the world, I spend the first hour or so on Monday morning explaining our mission and then exhorting the national pastors sitting in front of me to take the initiative in training others. When I tell them that it's up to them to reach their own nation for Christ by continuously raising up faithful men with the training they receive, they become very enthusiastic. In fact, in Africa, I have had standing ovations within the first hour of teaching, and that's before we even got started teaching! This kind of response demonstrates the importance of what we do when we actually equip indigenous leaders to reach their own nations. Far too many mission efforts have become mere reproductions of their Western founders, and in time that mission loses its relevance within the prevailing culture. I began to understand this when first teaching in Rwanda. The singing was always accompanied by some form of native dance. It's not dancing as we normally think of dancing but rather an art form of worship seldom seen in the West.

Last year in Liberia I saw another example of indigenous worship which I have never seen before. Just after class ended we drove out into the bush for about two hours. We drove through several unreached jungle villages until we reached our destination. It was a Christian village and the people were getting ready to prepare the evening meal for themselves and their guests. As we toured the village, I noticed a woman beating out locally produced rice in a huge vessel with an even larger wooden pestal. It was the most incredibly delicious rice I have ever eaten in my life.

After we ate, we had a time of singing and preaching. The singing was the most unique element of their worship. There was one woman leading a chorus while the remaining congregation echoed a response. It was repetitive and the sound was unlike anything I had ever experienced. The primary lines sung by the woman in the song were statements of truth about the promises of God. The congregation's response was an affirmation of the primary lyric and as they sang the song, they became more emphatic. By the time the song was finished they had entered into a full state of worship and adoration of God that was both authentic and humbling to all of us present. Preaching the word of God in such an environment as that is a simple and powerful transition!

Why do I say all this? Because this native authenticity in life and worship is not something that is taught or passed on by Western missionaries or other ethnically diverse Christians. It's part of the indigenous culture where Christian faith already has found a welcome home. Our job as those outside the culture is not to do for the nationals what they can do for themselves, but rather to facilitate growth by helping them reproduce themselves consistent with the teaching of 2 Tim 2:1-7 and other key missions passages in the NT. Because indigenous leaders already know the language, understand how to work within the existing culture, and love the people around them, our training them equips and empowers nationals to do the ministry of Jesus Christ the most effectively of anyone on the planet.

The national pastors and other leaders with whom we have worked deserve and even demand that, once they have successfully acquired the knowledge necessary for building and maintaining expanding church ministries, they are the ones to most effectively advance their own churches and cultures through their own efforts. Even secular African leaders like Paul Kagame of Rwanda are rejecting the old patterns of foreign aid which offered wealth and progress not to the populace but to the client regimes who controlled them.[1] This same mindset must be modeled in the training of indigenous leaders who require self-directed autonomy to function best within their living environs.

Since 1994, Kagame has led Rwanda from the devastation of genocide to becoming one of the best examples of national resurgence on the continent. I can personally confirm this burgeoning posture in nations like Rwanda. This is evident even at street level in Kigali, the capital where we hold classes for the Baptist Union of Churches. Since I often have to go into the money exchange businesses to get local currency I am aware how white Westerners attract beggars and panhandlers of all kinds. In the past few years I have seen less and less of them upon emerging from the exchanges and even when a local approaches me to ask for money they are oftentimes rebuked by others around them for doing so. This is a simple reflection of the inherent pride found within indigenous leaders who know best how to reach their respective cultures with the gospel.

1. Moyo, *Dead Aid*, xix.

## Adopting a Long-Term Plan

No two churches are exactly alike and consequently no two missions programs are identical in the way they fund worldwide ministry. I have preached in hundreds of evangelical churches and have seen hundreds of other church's mission programs either up close or at a distance. Until either a pastoral staff or the missions committee or both do an assessment of what is being done, little will change if change is necessary. An assessment should probably be focused on at least three or four major areas.

First, any major checkup ought to begin with a philosophy of ministry. This answers key questions such as:

Are we operating with a true New Testament missions philosophy?

In reality this is a much tougher question than it may appear to be. Most pastors and mission committees may already think that they are already hitting the nail on the head in this area. An objective analysis is difficult for any organization to do because the initial reaction might be to just shrug the shoulders and admit victory instead of defeat. For some reason the old adage, "we just ain't never done it that way before" is a much more prevalent response in many established churches than we may be willing to admit. The older model may depend primarily, not exclusively, on sending mission couples to establish churches either among unreached people groups or to needy areas within countries with an evangelical gospel presence already established.

However, if the church has more contemporary roots, it may reflect more of a short-term missions team philosophy which focuses more on meeting temporal needs in order to build bridges for gospel communication among the unreached. As we have already seen, some contemporary churches have chosen service-oriented missions which do not include a dynamic gospel component. Other contemporary mission applications may simply be to provide services (such as digging wells, building structures, etc.) for Christian groups in a country in order to edify and encourage them in their present ministries. There can be myriad combinations of missions and mission activity that is all done under the rubric of the Great Commission of Jesus Christ among his churches.

The greatest question is whether what a church is doing ultimately fits the biblical model of the Great Commission. We must ask whether or not we are actively making disciples among all nations who are in turn making disciples. That is a yes or no question with no room for maybe or hope so. That is the essence of the key passages in Matt 28:18-20, Mk 16:15, Luke 24:47, Acts 1-28, and 2 Tim 2:1-7. All of these passages, or books (in the case of Acts), reveal that evangelizing and training must be the central components of any and every mission. These are the non-negotiables.

Therefore, if anything the church does is not aimed at and directly tied to these core values then no matter how "good" those extra activities might be they should be weeded out. It is very easy for the "good" things we do to become too important, and in fact they can even begin to challenge or even supplant Christ's core values. This can happen with the good things of soup kitchens, food pantries, pregnancy centers, etc. These are legitimate and helpful outreaches but they have to remain a means to the end of making disciples and not become an end in themselves. This requires vigilance from those who oversee the mission outreach of a local church. A second element that we must include in our assessment of how our mission activity fits the missions statement of the church's overall ministry. We then need to answer a second question:

## Are we fulfilling the primary goal of planting new churches?

The answer should be able to demonstrate that the present missions goal is directly connected to the mission of the church itself, which in turn is rooted in the Great Commission. In other words, whatever the church is attempting to do in its own *Jerusalem* ought to be identical with or at least reflect what it is attempting to do in its Judea, Samaria, and uttermost part in applying its central purpose. If there is a disconnect here than that means that money is probably being directed into certain kinds of ministry that don't fit the overall ministry portfolio. The greatest way to spread the gospel anywhere is to plant a church. In our Western culture we have an early history of revival among an earnest Christian community. This has been true all the way up through the twenty-first century. From Jonathan Edwards, Whitefield, all the way through the revival-driven nineteenth and twentieth centuries, Americans have been blessed with being connected to great spiritual movements which have swept millions of souls into the kingdom. The only drawback to many of the great American revivals was the lack of local church support and multiplication which did not follow in the wake of personal spiritual renewal. This was especially true of the D. L. Moody and Billy Sunday campaigns. It was also a concern with the Billy Graham revivals all over the world. What we lacked by way of local churches was often replaced in part by Christian organizations which attempted to meet specific spiritual and social needs that churches were not meeting. The lingering gap of fresh new local churches to evangelize growing urban areas has left a huge spiritual hole to fill all over America.

It is gratifying to see that many of the stronger Evangelicals have recognized this and responded, particularly among the Southern Baptist Convention. There are several stellar organizations who are addressing the need for training church planters and assisting them in building churches in strategic urban areas of the country. There are also several independent organizations who are doing similar ministry nationwide.

It would be tempting here for a Western evangelical church to rush to a parachurch entity to work through in performing its ministry, and that may be possible in some cases, but it may short-circuit the disciple-making process once people have been delivered from perilous situations. If they don't have the follow-up of a local church body who can minister to them, disciple them, and assist them in re-adjusting back into productive lifestyles we may essentially orphan them spiritually. Had the great soul-winning revivals of the D. L Moody, Billy Sunday, and Billy Graham ministries assimilated their millions of new believers into vibrant biblically oriented churches the evangelical movement may have looked somewhat different today.

When the home church commences a church planting effort in a *Samaria* or *uttermost part* area of the globe, this kind of outreach must commit itself to reaching and training nationals who will have the burden of reaching their respective areas with the gospel. That means that as we send personnel to start new church plants in places like Thailand or Cambodia those church plants must be prepared to aggressively disciple, train, and send out those they reach for Christ.

## Is there a reasonable balance between sending personnel and training locals?

Another important factor of the church's mission program is how the church drives its own disciple-making process. If training nationals is the ultimate goal of why we send our personnel and resources then we must remain focused on balancing efforts at both *reaching* nationals and *training* nationals.

Reaching nationals is the fundamental goal of any missions outreach. As we support a missionary person or team we're attempting to evangelize an unreached people group. This can happen anywhere and as we pursue that goal on a more distant mission field we may send personnel directly to that location to begin a new church. The greatest way to evangelize any new and unreached group is by establishing a church plant. The book of Acts is a showcase for this ecclesial strategy. In Paul's day, within a little more than seventy years, the gospel had reached the known world and beyond. Churches established in every territory became the means for advancing Christianity deep into succeeding generations. When existing believers are not locally present we must be prepared to send those whom God calls for specific areas of service to the unreached.

However, this is the most costly method of moving and advancing the gospel. It takes considerable resources to support and maintain non-native missionary families on the field. There are considerable cost differences between supporting nationals and

Western personnel. For instance, in Western Europe the costs can be far greater ($7,500-$9,500 a month) than they would be for the same family in a developing country in Africa ($4,500-$6,500 a month). These are average costs based on the number of children, etc., but remember these expenses have to be maintained for many years while the missionary is learning the language, learning to navigate the culture, and then ultimately engaging that culture in evangelism and the beginning of a church plant, not to mention raising his family. It may take upward of ten years to perhaps twice that long for a strong reproducing church to be established and leaders to be trained who are capable of training others perpetually. Added to that would be the sticker shock to simply maintain personnel on the field as opposed to assisting national workers. The national trainer who represents GBTF training other nationals in East Africa operates quite well on about $250 to $350 per month.

Obviously, the need for well-prepared nationals is especially needed in the 10/40 window area where millions of people live, work, and die without ever hearing the gospel once. Without a supply of indigenous men and women to train others, we should thank God that he is faithfully calling and placing workers from the outside into key areas of this specific geography. Many of these 10/40 natives are ardently resistant to the Christian gospel and actively persecute believers. National religions in both Buddhist, Hindu, and Muslim countries make it extremely difficult for Christians to live and work in peace.

GBTF has been teaching national pastors in Myanmar for over six years. Even though Christianity was introduced here in 1812, two hundred years later Buddhism remains a dominant faith, controlling nearly 90 percent of the populace. Our hosts in Yangon tell us repeatedly that the only hope for Myanmar is the ongoing training of more and more indigenous Christians to reach their people one-by-one. But even these Christian nationals are not without danger from Buddhist animosity and their determination to hold political and social power. In the northern provinces average estimates suggest that in 2017 over ten thousand Rohingya

Muslims had been killed by the Rakhine Buddhists, and that about 700,000 Rohingya are presently living in exile in neighboring Bangladesh or India. The UN has declared the case to be one of textbook ethnic cleansing. Despite this kind of opposition, native Christians are much advantaged over outsiders in being able to reach their own people with God's truth.

Church planters need to focus their attention on building reproducing churches as rapidly and as efficiently as possible in an environment of persecution. That should never mean that evangelism is limited to only a certain "target audience" but that house churches will be able to multiply themselves readily through a well-thought-out leadership plan. A strategy must involve intentionality in identifying the cultural and spiritual qualities required in the lives of those who start and then lead churches. After all, evangelism in succeeding generations will depend on how that process begins in the first generation.

Veteran missionary and author of *The Insanity of God*, Nik Ripkin identified five primary qualities of leadership for those living in countries where persecution exists; however these qualities transcend raising up churches among just oppressed believers. By his own admission these qualities also answered this question: *Through whom does truth travel the most quickly within any given culture?*

Here are the five cultural qualities carefully observed by Ripkin and others over years of missionary service.

1. Leaders will generally be male.

2. Leaders will generally be over thirty years of age.

3. Leaders will generally be married.

4. Leaders will generally be employed.

5. Leaders will generally have status in the community.[2]

Statistics demonstrate that when nationals that bear these distinctions are brought to Christ the probabilities of church planting

2. Ripkin, *The Insanity of Obedience*, 270.

success are significantly heightened among the indigenous. Those individuals who fit this profile also will more likely promote the sort of perpetual training outlined in 2 Tim 2. Furthermore, once we have invested in sending church-supported personnel to *reach* nationals who fit this model, great potential exists for these nationals to be trained to then assume *full responsibility* of reaching their own populaces. After we have reached key individuals in the culture it then becomes possible on any mission field to begin the secondary mission focus of *training* the nationals.

Once GBTF was launched in 2012, we became aware of just how many individuals and organizations exist for the purpose of either assisting or training indigenous leaders globally. In some areas in both East and West Africa we encounter multiple organizations who offer various forms of teaching, practical helps, along with organizations like ours who do nothing but labor toward identifying and assisting nationals in some area of training. In our hemisphere, Haiti serves as an example of these kinds of efforts. There are countless numbers of churches, organizations, and people who serve in Haiti every year. However, because of the systemic spiritual and economic poverty, along with the deeply entrenched corruption of the political class, Haiti will likely continue as a crippled nation for the foreseeable future.

In our own case, no example in the GBTF program provides a better example than that of the Rwanda classrooms. There, as I shared earlier, Global Baptist Training Foundation began the training of pastors within the Baptist Union of Churches in 2012. These pastors were mostly handpicked in the aftermath of the 1994 genocide to replace those who had been massacred. They had never received any preparation other than what they received within their own local churches under their now deceased pastors. Despite this lack of training many of them led larger congregations of upward of 1,500 people or more. Consequently, when GBTF arrived eighteen years after their installation as pastors, they were thrilled that God was giving them the kind of biblical preparation necessary to take their ministries to the next level. Today they are standing on the threshold of accomplishing far greater things than they ever thought possible just six years ago. The many years of annual training they have received have now taken on a providential perspective as the Rwandan government in late 2018 required academic credentials of the clergy. The government has clearly overextended its authority there, but like it or not, these Rwandan pastors now have valuable ministry credentials which didn't exist for them seven years ago!

In Liberia, a major transformation of a large evangelical group is presently underway in the interior. When GBTF began here in 2017, it was apparent that our native host and these Baptist pastors he helps direct were ready for seriously investing in their theological and biblical training. The foundation has nearly completed level one of the multi-level training system with about sixty nationals. In the course of training these Liberian pastors, GBTF has simultaneously partnered with Advance, a church planting organization who assists and finances African, East Asian, and Mexican church planters for one year at $50 US a month. Our agreement with this church planting powerhouse is that they will only support nationals who have been trained or are undergoing classroom instruction with GBTF. We have simply been amazed at what God is doing with the partnership of our two organizations.

In 2018 and 2019, one hundred new churches have been started in Liberia alone by the nationals who are currently being trained by GBTF. In one of the church plants I spoke in last year the young church planting national had already reached seventy-five people within six months, and on the morning I spoke there were six more conversions. In 2019, Global Baptist Training Foundation's church planting partner from Advance ministries spoke in the same church with 125 in attendance with twenty more conversions to Christ. This new church plant in the interior of Liberia with these cumulative results has been accomplished by a trained indigenous pastor with $50 US support a month in less than one calendar year! These same types of results are presently being repeated in Africa, East Asia, and Mexico. Except for exceptional cases, this kind of multiplication among national pastors is simply not a likely scenario with Western missionary personnel who struggle with language and cultural barriers, and whose maintenance costs run in the thousands each month. Many Western mission families will never produce these kinds of results in many years of being maintained on the field by hundreds of churches giving thousands of dollars.

In reality Global Baptist Training Foundation and ministries like our own are actually witnessing God's long-term mission plan materialize right in front of our eyes. What we are seeing happen is precisely what Paul had commanded of Timothy. His ultimate commission was to train *faithful men* who in turn would *train others* just like themselves. I believe that God's purpose in this plan was not just to perpetuate the Christian faith. If that was the case, there would have been no built-in element guaranteeing that the faith would expand numerically. But God's plan actually incorporates both concepts of perpetuity and subsequent numerical growth. Not only will the faith move forward into the next generation under this strategy, it will insure the multiplication of people embracing that faith.

Don't let the fact miss you that the book of Acts in the NT begins with a single congregation in Jerusalem throttled by persecution and problems, but by the time we reach the final chapter we become witnesses to the expansion of churches stretching all the way to Rome which included multiplied thousands of believers. None of the fundamentals of this geographic and numerical expansion are necessarily different today from the first century. The Jerusalem church was built with Jewish and Gentile converts who had deep roots in the synagogues, but think how different the church of Philippi looked to these Jewish-oriented believers. This church was started by Paul at a local riverside prayer meeting with a foreign woman named Lydia, a former demon-possessed woman, and a local jailor!

Consequently, every church is not going to look the same and that is to be expected in the planting of new churches. God burdens those with special backgrounds, gifts, and life experiences in every church to serve in uniquely important ways. Since churches are simply assemblies of everyday people we should no more expect cookie cutter *churches* than we do *people* anywhere in the world.

In each city across Asia, Paul and Barnabas "appointed elders for them in every church" (Acts 14:23). In Crete the apostle commanded Titus to "appoint elders in every town" (Titus 1:5). There are key factors here that demonstrate that Paul's apostolic method mirrors exactly what he later outlined in 2 Tim 2 to Timothy while he labored in Ephesus.

*First*, elders were recognized and set apart from all others for the express purpose of church leadership. The term elder indicates itself a person of gravity, maturity, and leadership qualifications which set them apart from all others. According to 2 Tim 2, the basis of these qualifications is *faithfulness* to Christ in the midst of rigorous spiritual service.

*Secondly*, they were local individuals from the area who likely identified ethnically or racially within the populace. This makes perfect sense especially when it involves the comfort level of someone hearing the gospel for the very first time. A person like this will more readily trust someone who looks and talks like them versus a foreigner who does not represent their own cultural values. As a former church planter in a neighboring English-speaking country I can personally attest to this issue despite the fact that my congregation looked and talked like me. I was forced to recognize that their culture was unique and required its own level of recognition and respect despite how much it appeared to be like my own!

*Thirdly*, they also would have spoken the local dialect or regional language. Nobody can duplicate the native colloquialisms better than those who use them, and at the end of the day communication is all about speaking to a person, not at them! Nationals are able to present the gospel fluently and readily wherever they might be, and this is a tremendous strategic advantage for the gospel.

*Finally*, local elders would have known the culture and would have been both knowledgeable and comfortable with the way that life was lived there. Taking the gospel into the future by training nationals fully incorporates each of these factors in God's global mission plan. Both *reaching* and *training* nationals is the fundamental key in rapidly and successfully moving and multiplying the gospel forward. This is precisely what our efforts must be in the 10/40 window where millions of unreached people live and die every day. Nationals can reach nationals effectively because there are no language, cultural, or relational stumbling blocks to the hearts of the unreached.

## What can our church do to become more missions-balanced in training nationals?

Every church is going to look at this issue differently. The real issue is understanding what you are effectively trying to do. If you are a member of the missions committee or board and need information, there are some things you need to do. First, the committee will need to determine the kinds of mission efforts you want to be involved in as a church. You might want to support a national pastor or several pastors. You need to make sure you know them. You need to make sure what their personal and ministry needs are before you commit to them. Depending on where they live, nationals do not need the kind of resources or the level of assistance a typical Western-style missionary requires to live and work.

Therefore you usually need someone in the know who can communicate effectively with them about their needs and their mission. Do they have a burden to reach their populations by reproducing leaders who will start churches? This is not information gained simply by asking them. Vetting requires good questions, and even better answers by your respective national missionary. Have you been able to vet them sufficiently to be assured of their integrity and faithful service? Once that is done, a church can determine support levels, duration of support, and how it will need to be administrated. Since you may not be working with a mission board or agency, you will have to know how to get money to them safely and securely.

There are always drawbacks to every support situation and there are some issues with which we must contend in training nationals everywhere. These servants of God will normally live on a much different level than we do here in America or in most developed countries. If a national is living in a developing country there is a good chance he comes from a country where systemic poverty and corruption abound. Our foundation works exclusively in developing countries like this and without exception life is predominately lived in these places at the survival level. Therefore, it is extremely tempting for even the best of God's servants to desire to completely remove all of the elements associated with a desperate lifestyle. In fact, to live above the cultural norm in a developing country is everyone's dream. The question that a supported national missionary must answer is just how much do they need so they can focus on the work God has called them to do? This is really no different than a person anywhere but it can create both personal and public issues in a culture where the majority have very little, especially in Africa.

It is incumbent on the supporting church to be keenly aware of any national they are attempting to directly support. It's not enough to know the culture, the church will have to do the necessary homework in knowing the missionary. This will require face-to-face visits and an accountability system in place to make sure any national understands what is expected of them in lieu of support.

Pastors and other church personnel who often take mission trips to various mission fields can begin this process by visiting fields of interest and holding meetings with groups of national pastors. Once on the field they can communicate directly to nationals who are qualified to start new churches, evangelize, or work alongside those spearheading new ministries. Personally, I believe that funding should be reserved for those spearheading church planting in unchurched areas. When a Western church is vetting prospective nationals for support, local leaders under review should already have demonstrated previous church planting efforts, and have the respect of their peers on the field. This kind of investigation is absolutely necessary if you want to maintain a healthy and productive relationship with indigenous leaders over the long haul.

In our foundation, we have anywhere from three hundred to five hundred national pastors we are training per year all over the world. Many of these pastors are starting churches and receive $50 a month from our church planting partner who does nothing but raise funding for this endeavor. This is not enough for most of them to live on per month but it allows them to know that they can put food on their tables while launching a church plant. This is all the vast majority of them essentially need. The GBTF East African trainer we have previously mentioned will begin holding Global Baptist Training Foundation classrooms in several East African nations by 2020, and we will handle his living support while he serves as a national trainer. This allows supporting and prospective churches to know that a reputable 501(c)(3) organization is handling and dispensing donations properly under direct accountability. We have several churches and individuals who are contributing toward this kind of personal ministry endeavor.

Churches may also want to work through missionary training organizations who travel to fields of interest and train nationals directly. There are many such organizations and each of them provide various levels of expertise in ministry training. Some are focused on more practical training geared to provide hands-on preparation for key church ministry areas . Others like Global Baptist Training Foundation offer extensive theological training which equips national pastors on a similar level in which American pastors and church leaders are trained in a Bible college or seminary. We are convinced that since less than 2 percent of all our national pastors have had any substantive training at all, this model is the most attractive and useful to the majority of indigenous leaders. Since 2012, nationals in over ten nations have independently reached out seeking theological equipping for ministry from GBTF on little more than just word of mouth. This trend will likely continue.

We envision that within the next decade our own organization will be training nationals in no less than twenty-five African states and duplicating nationals who will be independently training their own countrymen in each of them. This number does not include or anticipate the combined efforts of sister organizations who will likely expand efforts in their realms of service and influence. Furthermore, this is only Africa. Mexico, Central America, South America, India, Philippines, Korea, and a host of other countries have pockets of indigenous believers, large and small, who are waiting to be trained and sent out to reach their neighbors with the gospel.

Our collective hope is that there will be a shift in emphasis among a vast majority of gospel-centered churches who are seriously focused on moving and multiplying the gospel into the next generation. This fresh approach, while remaining committed to reaching the untold, must take advantage of the countless thousands of nationals who await the training and equipping they require to minister where they live. This latent yet powerful multitude of believers has the potential to exponentially increase Great Commission results.

Just recently as I was teaching in Rwanda I told the men that the commission of Christ to evangelize the world belonged just as much to them as it does every church in America. We serve the same gracious God who is no respecter of persons, and his power is readily available to those who desire to obey him by faith. While looking deep into their faces I could see how this message was slowly taking root and being believed among them. When I was finishing my short speech they applauded. I instantly realized that they weren't clapping for my oratory, but for themselves. Perhaps for the first time since they had themselves been reached with the gospel, they realized that not only were they responsible to multiply it, but also had the same God behind them awaiting their response to the gospel call to go themselves.

In October of 2019, I taught our second yearly classroom in Liberia in a new teaching site interior. I decided to invite our Rwandan trainer, Fidele Shinga, to join me so I could observe him teaching and share a word at times during the week of class. To be honest, I did not know what the chemistry would be like among these pastors from West Africa being taught by one of their brothers from East Africa. I have enough experience doing what I do to know that cultural differences can sometimes be quite small and yet become very important in critical communication. What I observed was both powerful and electrifying. Fidele began to tell the Liberian pastors about genocide and how he had survived as a young man. He shared the horrors of the three-month nightmare and how it ultimately changed him and his country.

Fidele went on and shared with them how, just twenty-five years this side of the country's near demise, Rwanda is fast becoming the new jewel of Africa. The men listened, asked questions, and shared some of their own stories of the Liberian civil wars which had decimated their own country. The camaraderie which developed in that room over the next several minutes was something beyond description. I was so enraptured myself with what I was witnessing that I forgot to pull out my phone and video the event! Nevertheless, once the Liberian pastors began to tell Fidele how God was working among their ranks to launch new churches with trained men all over their country, I instantly knew that Fidele would be taking this news back to Kigali to challenge his own brethren with the need to think bigger and better.

Africa is at a crossroads, just like many continents and countries before them. Change has come in many different forms both politically, socially, and spiritually. This is becoming increasingly true in the 10/40 window nations where so much of the world's unreached populations exist without the gospel. In Myanmar where we are presently training nationals to reach their nation, many of their own people need to hear the gospel of Christ. Nationals reaching nationals is the best way, the most expedient way, and the most economical way of moving and multiplying the gospel forward. Whenever and wherever we meet indigenous believers they tell us over and over again that they have recognized this but have lacked the training and equipping necessary to fulfill their destiny. The time has come to make the training of nationals the second blade of our two-edged missions sword. It needs to be sharpened and wielded.

# Conclusion

YOU MAY REMEMBER AS we began this book the story of the hockey player whose life was spared in a potentially tragic on-ice incident a few years ago. Fortunately, because the cardiac specialist, who was providentially on the ice that day, was able to save his life, his congenital issue was later able to be repaired, and his future is brighter than his wife, children, family, and friends could have ever hoped.

I often think of this story as I teach nationals around the globe in the very places they grew up, live, and will eventually die. They are God's providential servants on the scene to minister to the needs of their countrymen. Because they already know the language, understand and identify with the culture around them, and love those who live there, they are potentially the best equipped servants to reach the population with the gospel of Jesus Christ. They were born, live, and will eventually end their Christian service dwelling among their own people.

Every church of Jesus Christ needs to pursue a balanced program in reaching their world for Christ. The missions endeavor demands a balance between *reaching* nationals and then ultimately *training* them to reach their own populations for Christ. Because of over two hundred years of faithful missionary investment, many nations have believers scattered throughout them who need to be equipped and empowered for service. In many places it is no longer necessary to treat these geographical areas as if they were unreached by sending in outside personnel at significant expense. Missions programs focused on this exclusive model are oftentimes spending the bulk of their budgets doing so, and then getting limited returns on their mission dollars. If you are a pastor or a missions committee member I want to challenge you to reconsider your missionary budget because when already present, training and equipping nationals has proven that this method can produce optimal results! In the case of Liberia where we train over 150 indigenous pastors and have seen one hundred new church plants begun in just over one year, the pastors have committed themselves to a new national goal of launching five hundred new churches across the country by 2021. I wouldn't bet against them.

# Bibliography

Finley, Bob. *Reformation in Foreign Missions: A Call for Change in the Way Foreign Missionary Work Is Carried Out by Evangelical Christians.* Longwood, FL: Xulon, 2005.

Grudem, Wayne, and Barry Asmus. *The Poverty of Nations.* Wheaton: Crossway, 2013.

Johnson, Todd. "Christianity in its Global Context, 1970–2020: Society, Religion, and Mission." International Bulletin of Missionary Research 37, no. 3 (April 2013): 164. http://www.internationalbulletin.org/issues/2013-03/2013-03-164-editors.html.

Lupkin, Robert D. *Toxic Charity.* New York: Harper Collins, 2011.

Moyo, Dambisa. *Dead Aid: Why Aid is Not Working and How There is a Better Way for Africa.* New York: Farrar, Straus & Giroux, 2009.

Ripkin, Nik. *The Insanity of Obedience.* Nashville: B & H Publishing, 2014.

World Evangelization Research Center. "An AD 2001 Reality Check." http://injesus.com/messages/content/316929.

Yohannan, K. P. *Come Let's Reach the World.* Carrollton, TX: GFA, 2004.